CW00467817

An Introduction to Netbooks and Cloud Computing

Robert Penfold

Bernard Babani (publishing) Ltd
The Grampians
Shepherds Bush Road
London W6 7NF
England

www.babanibooks.com

Please note

Although every care has been taken with the production of this book to ensure that any projects, designs, modifications, and/or programs, etc., contained herewith, operate in a correct and safe manner and also that any components specified are normally available in Great Britain, the Publisher and Author do not accept responsibility in any way for the failure (including fault in design) of any projects, design, modification, or program to work correctly or to cause damage to any equipment that it may be connected to or used in conjunction with, or in respect of any other damage or injury that may be caused, nor do the Publishers accept responsibility in any way for the failure to obtain specified components.

Notice is also given that if any equipment that is still under warranty is modified in any way or used or connected with home-built equipment then that warranty may be void.

© 2010 BERNARD BABANI (publishing) LTD

First Published - February 2010

British Library Cataloguing in Publication Data

A catalogue record for this book is available from the British Library

ISBN 978 0 85934 712 9

Cover Design by Gregor Arthur

Printed and bound in Great Britain for Bernard Babani (publishing) Ltd

Portable PCs of one kind or another have been in existence for many years, but until quite recently they sold in relatively small numbers. It is easy to see why this should be, with a typical laptop or notebook having a mediocre specification and a high asking price. There were actually some laptop PCs that had quite impressive specifications by the standards of the day, but they were so expensive as to be well beyond the reach of the average PC user. Things have moved on, and sales of laptop PCs surpassed those of desktop PCs in 2005, and have strengthened further since then.

I suppose that the recent upsurge in the popularity of netbook PCs is really just a continuation of the trend started by notebook and laptop PCs. The obvious conclusion from the sales data is that large numbers of people need to use a computer while away from home or the office, and that small, lightweight PCs are preferred to the larger and heavier types even if this means making a few changes to the way in which the computer is used.

While this is certainly true, it is not the whole story. Large numbers of portable PCs are sold to people who will mainly or exclusively use them as normal home or even small office PCs. I would certainly not claim that a netbook PC was suitable for use as the main PC for a small office, but many people requiring a PC for tasks such as shopping online, writing the occasional letter, and checking Email happily use a netbook as their sole computer. Provided you are comfortable using the small keyboards and screens of these computers, it is possible to use them to run a wide variety of application programs. When you have finished using a netbook it can be stored away out of sight in even the smallest of cupboards or drawers.

Probably the vast majority of netbook users buy their computers for use on the move, and, again provided you can live quite happily with the small screen and keyboard; it is capable of handling most of the tasks performed by laptops and notebooks. However, a netbook is a fraction of the size and weight of these other portable PCs, and the battery life is usually very much better. Netbooks are genuinely portable, and are a practical proposition if it is necessary to carry a computer around with you all day.

While using a netbook PC is to some extent the same as using a desktop type, there are plenty of differences as well. A modern netbook PC usually has a sizeable built-in hard disc drive, making it possible to run most of your normal application programs if you should decide to do so. However, most netbook users opt for the alternative approach of using free online services, which is a form of "cloud" computing. Whether you will use a netbook at home, on the move, with conventional software or for cloud computing, this book will help you to decide on a suitable model. It will also help you to get your new netbook PC set up properly and working efficiently.

Robert Penfold

Trademarks

Microsoft, Windows, Windows XP, Windows Vista, and Windows 7 are either registered trademarks or trademarks of Microsoft Corporation.

All other brand and product names used in this book are recognised trademarks, or registered trademarks of their respective companies. There is no intent to use any trademarks generically and readers should investigate ownership of a trademark before using it for any purpose.

Contents

3

Cloud computing 91

Choosing
a netbook

Netbook?

Before getting properly under way with this book it would probably be as well to define precisely what we mean by a "netbook". I suppose that the question "what is a netbook" is very much a "how long is a piece of string" type of question. Due to the current popularity of notebook computers we have a situation where some retailers and manufacturers try to call practically any portable computer as a netbook. The definition of a netbook computer is to some extent a matter of opinion, but there are some characteristics which a computer must have in order to fit into this category.

The idea of a netbook is to provide the user with a computer that is small and light even by laptop and notebook standards, but it's powerful enough to enable most everyday computing tasks to be undertaken. In fact the first netbooks were primarily intended as a "proper" way of accessing Email systems and the Internet, without the compromises involved with other portable Internet devices. It is from this that the "net" part of the name is derived. However, these days netbooks are used as much more than a means of accessing Emails and the Internet while on the move.

First and foremost, the notebook computer must have a relatively small screen, but not one as diminutive as those found on digital gadgets such as mobile phones and cameras. The upper limit is somewhere around the 10 inch mark, and much above that the computer is really into the realms of the notebook or laptop. Anything much less than about 7 inches is unlikely to be of much practical use in real-world computing.

In terms of raw computing power I think it is fair to say that most notebook computers fall some way short of most laptop and notebook types, and they are certainly not in the same league as a typical desktop PC. Although this may seem like a major shortcoming, the computing power of a typical desktop PC is actually far greater than is needed for many everyday computing tasks such as surfing the Internet, word processing, and using a spreadsheet. Thus, even though a netbook computer may have a relatively slow microprocessor it is still capable of running most types of software.

It is helpful to bear in mind that the processor in a typical notebook computer is actually more powerful than those that were used in most desktop PCs only a few years ago. We happily used the desktop PCs of a few years ago in all manner of computing tasks without any difficulties, and it is certainly possible to run most types of software on a netbook PC. However, the small screen size and lack of raw processing power do impose some limitations, and with a netbook PC it might not always be possible to run the most up-to-date software. This is something that tends to be reflected in the operating systems used for the more basic netbook PCs. Operating systems that are out of date or even obsolete in the world of desktop PCs are in common use with netbooks that have a very basic specification.

Disc drives

It is really the disc drives that provide the most obvious difference between a netbook PC and a notebook or laptop type. It would perhaps be more precise to say that it is the lack of disc drives that provides the most obvious difference. Notebook and laptop PCs usually have a fairly high capacity hard disc drive, together with a drive that can read and write with most types of CD and DVD media. A netbook PC does not necessarily have any conventional disc drives at all.

Netbook PCs can really be divided into two distinctly different types. These are the ones that have a built-in hard disc drive and the type that does not. As one would probably expect, it is the larger netbook PCs that tend to have a built-in disc drive, and the really small and lightweight types that do not. Neither type has the space to accommodate any type of internal CD or DVD drive, but can be used with external units. The smaller netbook PCs therefore lack any form of conventional disc drive.

On the face of it, a PC that does not have a hard disc drive is of little practical use, since there is nowhere to store the operating system, data, or programs. PCs use a disc based operating system that is automatically booted when the unit is switched on, so without a disc drive there can be no operating system, and the computer cannot get beyond the start-up testing routine. However, instead of using a hard disc drive these really small netbook computers utilise Flash memory. Like a hard disc drive, and unlike normal computer memory, Flash memory does not lose its contents when the power is switched off. This makes it possible to use Flash memory in exactly the same way as a hard disc drive.

Flash memory has the advantage of being relatively small, light, and requiring little power, but it is relatively slow and the capacity is usually well below that of typical portable hard disc drives. In recent years there have been big improvements in the speed of Flash memory, and although it is still generally slower than a typical hard disc drive, it is perfectly adequate in this respect. The cost of this type of memory has fallen massively in recent years, making it a practical proposition to have quite large Flash drives.

Even so, Flash drives in low-cost netbooks tend to be very much "second best" when compared to a hard disc type. The hard disc drives in modern portable PCs often have a capacity in excess of 100 GB, and the capacity is unlikely to be less than 40 GB. A netbook that relies on Flash memory has to typically make do with just a few gigabytes of disc capacity, although there is usually the option of augmenting this somewhat by using Flash memory cards. A netbook Flash drive typically has about one tenth of the capacity of a netbook hard disc drive. This is insufficient to run a modern desktop version of Windows.

The situation is very different with a netbook PC that has a hard disc drive. A netbook computer equipped with a hard disc drive should be capable of running any normal PC operating system, and practically any PC application software as well. Furthermore, it should be possible to load numerous application programs onto the drive. If you wish to use it that way, a netbook of this type can be used in much the same way as a laptop or notebook PC.

The same is not true for a netbook computer that has to rely on a few gigabytes of Flash memory. Only older PC operating systems will run in such a small amount of space, or those that are specifically designed for use with this type of computer. It is unlikely that there will be much spare capacity for applications software. As explained later in this book, it is possible to use Internet resources to compensate to a large extent for the lack of hardware in a really small netbook PC. In fact this approach is often used even if a netbook does have a reasonable hard disc capacity. Using Internet resources helps to keep the hard disc free for when it is really needed, and can have other advantages as well. It also circumvents the problem of loading conventional software onto a computer that has no optical disc drive.

*Fig.1.1   The built-in microphone is on the left, and the webcam is just
to the right of centre*

Some of the more upmarket netbooks have a so-called solid state drive,
or SSD as it is sometimes termed. This is basically just a huge amount
of ultra-fast Flash memory, producing a drive that is comparable to a
hard disc type in terms of speed and capacity. A solid state drive has the
advantage of much reduced power consumption in comparison to any
hard disc drive. It is likely that in the future the cost of solid state drives
will reduce to the point where they will take over from hard disc types in
portable PCs, but at present they are too expensive to be a practical
proposition for most users. A netbook that has a solid state drive is used
in exactly the same way as one that has a hard disc drive.

The original netbooks were mainly of the smaller type with no hard disc
drive, but these days it is the slightly larger type with a built in hard disc
that are "selling like hot cakes". The smaller type are now often referred
to "minibooks" in order to make a clear distinction between the two types.
This book has primarily been written with the larger type of netbook in
mind, but the vast majority of it also applies to the minibook type.

The good and bad

Although the specifications of netbook PCs may be lacking in some
respects, they are quite good in others. There are normally audio
connectors for headphones and a microphone, making it possible to
use media players and dictation software that records your voice.
Unfortunately, the hardware requirements for modern voice recognition
software are well beyond the capabilities of many netbook computers.
This is a pity, since a combination of good voice recognition software
and a small portable computer is a very potent one.

An external WebCam is not needed with most netbook computers as
this facility is normally built-in. It is usually in the lid of the computer, just
above the screen (Figure 1.1 – right), making it easy to use. There may
well be an integral microphone as well (Figure 1.1 – left), but it is still

*Fig.1.2 An external optical drive is a very useful accessory for a
netbook user*

useful to have a microphone socket for use with a higher quality type or
if you wish to use a headset.

Ports

There will usually be at least two or three USB ports, enabling the
computer to be connected to a wide range of peripheral devices such as
printers, scanners, pointing devices, card readers, and digital cameras.
With no form of integral CD or DVD drive, one of the most useful peripheral
gadgets for use with a netbook PC is an external drive that can handle

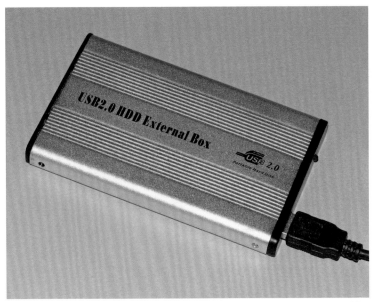

*Fig1.3 An external hard disc drive is useful as a backup device, and is
well worthwhile even if the netbook has a large built-in hard
drive*

CD and DVD media (Figure 1.2). One of these connected to a modern
USB port should be every bit as fast as an internal equivalent.

An external hard disc drive (Figure 1.3) connected to a USB is more than
a little useful with any PC that lacks a built-in hard disc drive or has one
of relatively small capacity. It can also be useful as a backup drive in
cases where the built-in drive has a fairly high capacity. However, there
are alternative methods of backing up your data, such as online data
storage, so an external drive is by no means essential.

Do not expect much in the way of ports beyond a few USB types. Modern
desktop computers tend to rely heavily on USB ports for expansion, with
the so-called legacy ports (RS232C serial, parallel printer, etc.) gradually
being phased out. This approach is fully implemented with netbook
PCs, which are unlikely to have any form of legacy port. It is still possible
to connect a netbook computer to older PC peripherals using a suitable
USB adaptor, such as the USB/RS232C serial type shown in Figure 1.4,
but with anything like this you have to bear in mind that there can be
problems with driver software for the peripheral gadget.

Fig.1.4 A USB adaptor can be used to provide legacy ports. This unit provides a standard RS232C serial port

Suitable drivers for the operating system used on your new netbook may not be available. Simply getting a device connected to a PC correctly is not enough, and without suitable driver software it will not be usable. The operating system will either fail to "see" the device at all, or it will report the gadget as not being installed correctly. Note that any software supplied with the adaptor will simply be the driver software to install the adapter as the appropriate type of port. Any peripheral gadget that is connected to the adaptor must be installed using its own driver program in the normal fashion. It is advisable to obtain suitable device drivers for the peripheral device prior to buying any sort of port adaptor, and to abandon the idea if the necessary driver software cannot be obtained.

Of course, it is unlikely that there will be any problems with the simpler and well standardised devices such as normal PS/2 mice and keyboards. When used with an appropriate USB adaptor, these will be recognised as USB mice and keyboards by the operating system, which will then install the standard driver software. It is the more complex devices that tend to be problematic, with scanners probably rating as the most troublesome type. Forget about trying to use a SCSI device such as a scanner with a netbook computer.

Networking

As with any portable PC, the normal way of using a netbook is to work "out and about" with it all day, and to then upload the accumulated data to a desktop PC or computer network at the end of the day. It is possible to link a netbook to other computers using a USB port, but this is not the most convenient way of doing things. There are better ways of networking, and this is one respect in which netbook PCs are usually well equipped. For the vast majority of users it is probably best to avoid netbooks that do not have good networking facilities.

There should be a standard Ethernet connector so that the computer can be hard-wired to a standard PC network. While I would always like this option to be available, using an Ethernet port is not the most convenient way of connecting a netbook PC to a network. Most netbook computers have a built-in wi-fi interface so that it is possible to connect to the network wirelessly. This is a much more convenient way of doing things since it avoids the need to keep plugging the computer into the network and unplugging it again, and in most cases it is possible to connect to the network from anywhere within the same building. In fact you can usually connect to the network in your house while sitting in the garden, or the shed at the bottom of the garden.

Note that some netbooks have a built-in Bluetooth adaptor, but Bluetooth and wi-fi are not the same. Both provide interconnections using radio signals rather than wires, but they are designed to fulfil different needs. Wi-fi is designed specifically as a means of implementing an Ethernet network without using cables. It will often be possible to use peripheral devices such as printers via the network, but these devices must be made available as shared network resources. Bluetooth is intended more as an alternative to USB, and it provides a general means of connecting to other gadgets. The connection is normally just from one gadget to another, such as a computer to a printer, and there is no network involved.

Internet connection

While it is possible to use a netbook without an Internet connection, a netbook PC on its own is a bit like a horse and cart without the horse. Most users will require a reasonably fast Internet connection in order to fully exploit their netbook's potential. This is not likely to be a problem when the computer is connected to your home network or a network at work. Either way, the network will usually have some sort of broadband Internet connection that can be shared by the computers in the system. Thus, when you connect a netbook to a network, whether using a wired or wi-fi connection, you will normally gain Internet access.

Wi-fi also provides Internet access via the numerous wi-fi "hotspots" around the world, although in most cases there is a charge for this service. It is also possible to connect to the Internet using a dial-up or broadband modem connected to a USB port. Although an ordinary dial-up modem is usually included as part of the internal hardware with laptop and notebook computers, it is not a universal feature with netbook PCs. In fact it seems to be something of a rarity. Many of the normal ways of using a netbook are dependent on a fast Internet connection, so it is possible that the manufacturers deem a dial-up connection to be inadequate. However, it could still be useful as an emergency standby. Anyway, simply connecting the computer to a telephone socket and using a dial-up connection might not be an option.

Another way of providing a netbook with an Internet connection is to use a wireless connection to a 3G mobile telephone service. This method of connecting to the Internet was ludicrously expensive in the early days of 3G telephone services. Downloading several gigabytes of data cost about the same as a new Ferrari! Competition and the poor initial take-up of 3G services have forced prices down to levels that are now much more reasonable, and can be comparable to other forms of broadband access.

An advantage of this method of connecting to the Internet is that it is available anywhere that the selected service is in-range. Bear in mind that the access speeds of 3G services are dependent on the quality of the signal obtained, and in general are significantly slower than other types of broadband connection. However, they are still much faster than ordinary dial-up connections, and are adequate for most purposes. Some netbooks have the necessary hardware built-in, and in order to get started it is merely necessary to install a SIM card. In most cases though, this type of connection must be made using a so-called broadband dongle, which is a small gadget that connects to a USB port. The dongle can usually be obtained as part of the broadband deal, and should be supplied with the necessary driver software, plus any other software that might be needed in order to use it properly. Note that driver software for Linux systems is not always available, so it is advisable to check this point before "signing on the dotted line" if your netbook runs under any version of Linux.

Monitor

The built-in monitor of a netbook PC usually offers reasonably high resolution and "crisp" picture quality with good colour rendition. Obviously some compromises have to be made with the screen resolutions of the really small netbooks, although the resolutions provided actually compare quite well with those of most desktop PCs from some years ago. There is clearly a huge advantage in having a large and very high resolution screen for some applications, such as photo-editing, and the small screen size of a netbook PC may preclude some applications from being used at all.

The larger netbooks usually have an ordinary VGA monitor output, as do some of the really small types. This enables the computer to be used with a large monitor when back at base. Obviously this feature will be of little use when working "out and about" with the netbook, but it is still useful to have this facility. A netbook computer is unlikely to have a DVI port to provide a digital video signal, but this is unlikely to be of any great practical importance. Most modern monitors have just a VGA input or both VGA and DVI types. Either way, there is a VGA input for use with a netbook computer. The picture quality obtained using an ordinary VGA port should be extremely good.

Most of the time it will not be possible to use an external monitor, and the small screen size of a netbook is a significant drawback. Those with excellent eyesight will probably be prepared to accept this drawback, but bear in mind that it is not a good idea to use a small screen for long periods. Something like a laptop computer with a 15 to 17-inch screen is a better option where it will sometimes be necessary to use the computer for a few hours at a time. A laptop or notebook PC might be the only practical option if your eyesight at short distances is not particularly good.

Expansion slot

Desktop PCs have various forms of PCI expansion slot for internal expansion, and there are numerous types of PCI card available covering common and more specialist requirement. Laptop and notebook PCs often have an expansion slot such as a PCMCIA type. The range of available expansion cards is not as vast as for PCI slots, but there is still a large selection to choose from. Netbook PCs sometimes have some form of expansion slot, but most lack provision for any form of expansion card.

Fig.1.5 The built-in pointing device is usually a fairly basic touch pad

This is not to say that a netbook PC is restricted to the facilities provided by its built-in hardware. The USB ports provide a means for expanding the computer's capabilities, and a huge range of USB add-ons can be obtained. External expansion is a less neat solution than using internal cards, but it is the only practical solution with a PC that is designed to be as small as possible. The internal expansion slots of portable PCs tend to be used very little these days, presumably because many popular types of expansion, such as wi-fi adaptors and memory card readers, are included as part of the standard specification. There is little point in making a netbook bigger in order to provide expansion cards slots that will never be used.

Pointing device

As with laptop and notebook computers, a netbook type invariably has some form of built-in pointing device such as a touchpad (Figure 1.5).

*Fig.1.6 The keyboard of a netbook inevitably involves several
compromises, including a relatively small number of keys*

Some of these are easier to use than are others, and to a large extent
this is a matter of personal preference. Using the built-in pointing device
is obviously a neater solution than using an external type, but a mouse
or other pointing gadget can be connected to a USB port if necessary. I
find the small touch pads on netbooks very difficult to use, and that being
encumbered with a mouse is well worth it due to the comparative ease
with which the computer can be used.

Having a full size keyboard on a tiny computer is very much a case of
trying "to fit quart into a pint pot", and a netbook PC will inevitably have
something well short of a full-size keyboard. Some people find small
keyboards easy to use, while others find it almost impossible to type
anything more than a few characters at the time. This is something where
it is advisable to "try before you buy" if at all possible. I find that my high-
speed one finger typing gives no problems with some netbook keyboards,
but it is virtually impossible with others. The small size of the keys presents
no problems, but keys that have a very limited travel invariably do so.
No doubt some others find that the opposite is the case.

The small size of a netbook keyboard is not only achieved by making
the keys slightly smaller than normal. As with the keyboards of notebook
and laptop computers, there are fewer keys as well. Additionally, some
keys of a netbooks keyboard are very much smaller than normal. The
keyboard of a 10.1-inch Acer netbook is shown in Figure 1.6.

On the top row this has a full set of twelve function keys, plus Escape, Delete, etc. However, in order to get everything in it has been necessary to make the keys tiny, and the same is true of the six keys in the cursor control section in the bottom right-hand corner of the keyboard. The idea is presumably to make these keys very small as they are used infrequently, so that the other keys can then be made larger and easier to use.

As with most laptop and notebook PCs, there is no separate numeric keypad. However, some of the keys in the right-hand section can be set to operate as a numeric keypad. Hence some of these keys are marked with more than one character. The J, K, and L keys for example, respectively act as the 1, 2, and 3 keys in the numeric keypad.

There are two problems with this compromise, one of which is simply that it is not possible to have the numeric keypad and the normal QWERTY keyboard at the same time. While this will often be of no consequence, in some circumstances it could be necessary to frequently switch from one mode to the other. The other problem is that a numeric keypad normally has the keys aligned vertically and horizontally, but using the ordinary keys results in a keypad with the keys in diagonal rows and columns. It could take a while to get used to this arrangement.

All or most of the function keys have special functions when used in conjunction with the Fn key, which is usually to be found between the Control and Alt keys. This is effectively a Shift key for the function keys. In this example the embedded numeric keypad is switched on by pressing the Fn and F11 keys, and switched off by pressing them again. Typical alternative uses for the function keys are switching the display on and off, switching the sound on and off, and controlling the brightness of the screen.

Of course, a normal PC keyboard can be connected to a USB port of the computer, but this is only likely to be of any practical use when back at base. Carrying a standard PC keyboard around with you is not really a practical proposition, and the keyboard is likely to be two or three times larger than the netbook computer itself. A notebook or laptop PC is probably a better choice if you really must have something approximating to a full-size keyboard.

Battery life

Probably the most common complaint from users of laptop and notebook PCs is that the battery does not last long enough. Here we are talking about the time it takes the battery to run down and require a recharge, and not the time it takes for the battery to cease working properly so that it has to be replaced. The claimed battery life for laptop and notebook computers is often three hours or more, but this usually assumes that the computer will only be used in applications that consume relatively little power. With real-world computing it can often take little more than an hour to exhaust a fully charged battery.

Much longer battery life is often claimed as a big advantage of netbook PCs. The reasoning behind this is based on the fact that the hardware of a netbook tends to consume much less power than the hardware of laptop and notebook PCs. Because the power consumption of a netbook PC is much less, the battery will therefore last much longer.

Unfortunately, this is a gross oversimplification that ignores the capacity of the battery. With a battery of a given size it is indeed true that a netbook computer should provide many more hours of use per charge than a laptop or notebook PC. However, in practice the size of the battery is often proportional to the size of the portable PC. Bigger computers consume more power, but they have larger batteries with much higher capacities.

Even so, netbook computers generally operate significantly longer per charge than notebook or laptop types. Some can operate for many hours on a single charge. Unfortunately, a few are not much better than in this respect than the larger portable PCs. It is important to carefully check this point in the specifications of any netbook PCs that you might buy if long battery life is an important factor. In general, it is the smallest netbooks with the most basic specifications that provide the best battery lives. Sometimes it is possible to obtain a higher capacity battery as an optional extra. The cost of a replacement battery is often quite high, and one having about twice the capacity of the standard type will probably be quite expensive. It could still be well worth the money if the netbook will be used a great deal while on the move, and bear in mind that the original battery will be available as a standby if the high-capacity one runs right down and you get "caught short".

Laptop or notebook?

The terms "laptop" and "notebook" seem to cause a certain amount of confusion these days, and the differences between the two have decreased over the years. In fact the differences have been eroded to the point that these two terms are largely interchangeable. However, in the context of this book it is probably best if a clear distinction is made

Fig.1.7 A notebook PC on top of a laptop type. The notebook PC is slightly smaller overall, and it is also lighter, but the difference is not immediately obvious

between the two. In the past, a laptop PC was substantially larger than a notebook type, and physically was much the same as a modern laptop. The technology has moved on over the years, and a modern laptop is better specified while perhaps being a bit lighter, but the general appearance and concept remain the same.

Notebook computers were significantly smaller than the laptop variety, but still had screens of reasonable dimensions and a proper QWERTY keyboard. This made them more portable, but made them relatively fiddly and difficult to use. In fact the notebook computers of some years ago were remarkably similar to modern netbook types. Netbook computing tends to be regarded as a new concept, but its origins can be traced back many years.

Modern notebook PCs have tended to grow in size, meaning that they are now little different to laptops. In fact some manufacturers do not differentiate between the two, and seem to use whichever term takes their fancy. This means that for most practical purposes there is no longer any difference between the two.

However, a few manufacturers do produce laptop and notebook PCs, with a slight difference between the two ranges. When closed, a notebook is a bit thinner than a laptop. The difference is not usually very great, but it apparently enables notebooks to fit into special compartments in some briefcases, camera bags, etc. A chunkier laptop will not always fit into one of these cases. Figure 1.7 shows the front view of a Dell laptop PC and an HP notebook type, both of which have 15.4-inch screens. The difference in height is not great, but the notebook PC is noticeably lighter than the laptop type.

Apart from the difference in size and weight there is little practical difference between the two types, although the smaller size of a notebook PC means that it is likely to have a slightly shorter battery life. When deciding whether to buy a laptop, notebook, or netbook PC it is important to clearly differentiate between the three types. A laptop PC is far larger and heavier than a netbook type, but the difference between a notebook and a netbook type is significantly less. A true notebook computer is therefore a more direct rival to a netbook type.

Netbook, notebook, or laptop?

When using any portable computer you have to accept at least a few compromises. The smaller and lighter the computer, the greater the degree of compromise. Using an upmarket laptop PC that has a 17-inch screen is not that much different to using a desktop PC, and I suppose it is possible that an expensive portable PC of this type could actually be better specified than a typical PC in some respects. At the other extreme, a tiny computer with no built-in hard disc drive will involve compromises in virtually every aspect of its use.

When buying a portable PC it is usually a matter of finding the best compromise between small size and weight on the one hand, and ease of use on the other. The best compromise depends on the particular user and the way in which the computer will be used. Small size and lightness are unlikely to be major considerations for someone driving from one client to another and using the computer to show some sort of presentation. The computer will only be carried short distances, and a relatively large screen would help to make the presentations look as impressive as possible. Battery life is unlikely to be a major consideration either, since it will often be possible to power the computer from the mains supply, and one or two spare batteries could easily be carried in the car.

Matters are much the same for someone who needs a computer for home use, but is not prepared to provide a permanent work area for it. A large laptop PC can be used on the kitchen table and then stored away in practically any drawer or cupboard when it is not in use. Battery life is not an important consideration because the computer will normally be powered from the mains supply using the adaptor that comes as standard with most laptop PCs.

The situation is very different for someone who will find it necessary to carry the computer for much of the day, perhaps stopping occasionally at any convenient place to take notes or store some facts and figures. Few people are prepared to carry a laptop PC or even one of the lighter notebook types for very long. Carrying one or two spare batteries is probably not a very practical proposition either, since most laptop batteries are quite large and heavy. A netbook PC that has a fairly long battery life is probably the only practical solution in a situation of this type.

Each user has to work out the best compromise for their particular situation and personal preferences. With portable computers it is very helpful to go to a shop and actually try out various types. If you simply find one with a likely looking specification and then buy online, you might find that it is actually a lot bigger and heavier than you expected, or that the screen and keyboard are so small that you find them impossible to use. Trying out a few netbooks in a shop should make it easy to find one that really suits your requirements, and should help to avoid costly mistakes.

Before deciding that a netbook will suit your requirements, take into consideration the lack of a built-in optical drive. If you will need to install programs from CDs or DVDs, or use them for data storage and retrieval, a suitable external drive will be needed. The added cost of this drive needs to be taken into account, since it can substantially boost the overall cost of the system. It might actually be possible to obtain a portable CD-ROM drive quite cheaply, and this will permit programs to be installed from CDs, audio CDs to be ripped to MP3 files, etc. However, anything beyond a simple CD-ROM drive is likely to be much more expensive.

Of course, there are ways of using a netbook without any form of optical drive, and this is probably the way that most people use them. This subject is given extensive coverage in the other two chapters of this book. The lack of an optical drive will be of no consequence if you are happy to use these alternative methods of working.

Fig.1.8 A modern word processor has a WYSIWYG display and can handle graphics such as photographs

Suitable applications

When choosing a portable computer you need to take into consideration the application programs that will be run on it. There is no point in buying a top-of-the-range laptop and then using it for undemanding tasks that a relatively simple and inexpensive netbook could easily handle. Equally, there is also no point in buying a very basic netbook and then trying to run high-end applications on it. Even if your application programs will actually run, they are unlikely to work in a really usable fashion.

Word processing

Modern word processors are more sophisticated than the early programs for the PC that were strictly text-only and had no graphics capability. Apart from some very basic programs that are really text editors, word processors that run under Windows provide WYSIWYG (what you see is what you get) displays. In other words, the text is displayed in the correct font, style, colour, and so on. Also, these programs can handle graphics elements of various types, such as diagrams, photographs, and charts (Figure 1.8).

The demands on the hardware vary enormously depending on the type of word processing that is undertaken. Little loading is placed on the processor when undertaking straightforward word processing that does not include any graphics content. A WYSIWYG text display requires much more processing power than a basic text-only screen, but it is something that any reasonably specified netbook should be able to handle with ease.

For this type of thing it is not even essential to buy any word processor software. The WordPad program built into Windows (Start – All Programs – Accessories – WordPad) is suitable for basic word processing. However, for anything other than fairly basic word processing tasks it is advisable to obtain some good quality software. Most Linux installations include some fairly sophisticated word processing software as standard.

If a netbook is needed for taking notes, and even if large amounts of text will be accumulated, a fairly basic type should be more than sufficient. One of the larger netbooks is adequate for more serious word processing that has no more than a small amount of graphical content. For word processing that includes a fair amount of graphics it might be better to opt for a mid-range laptop that has a fairly large screen (15 inches or more).

Although a netbook is in many ways ideal for taking notes when on the move, it does, of course, have a major drawback. A full-size QWERTY keyboard is a definite advantage in any application that requires large amounts of text to be entered. A netbook does have a QWERTY keyboard, but as pointed out previously, it will inevitably be significantly smaller than a normal PC keyboard. Some people find a small keyboard easy to use, while others find one unusable for entering anything more than a few words. Each individual has to make up their own mind on this point.

DTP

DTP (desktop publishing) software has similar requirements to the word processing variety. A significant amount of word processing work actually entails using the program as a sort of pseudo DTP type. The difference between these two types of program has become blurred in recent years. In general though, DTP programs provide more control over page layouts and require more processing power and memory in order to run really well.

Using a DTP program to do page layouts that only contain text is not very demanding on the hardware, and any reasonably up-to-date netbook should be able to handle it. More complex DTP work that involves a significant graphical content requires something more powerful such as an upmarket laptop. The small screen of a netbook is a major drawback in DTP applications, especially where large and complex pages are involved. For anything other than simple page layouts a netbook is far from ideal.

Business applications

Other standard business applications such as databases and spreadsheets do not require a particularly powerful PC. Bear in mind that the use of graphics will place higher demands on the processor. Some types of graphics require a reasonably large screen, but in other respects any netbook should be able to handle standard business programs.

CAD

CAD stands for computer aided design or computer aided drawing, and it is software primarily used for producing technical drawings (Figure 1.9). This usually means a plan for something, such as a house extension, some house wiring, a piece of electronics, or an item of furniture. Producing two-dimensional drawings is not demanding on the processor, but a large screen is needed when producing complex drawings. A 15 to 17-inch screen is adequate for many types of drawing, so a laptop with a large screen is just about suitable for some two-dimensional CAD work, but a netbook with its 7 to 10-inch screen is far from ideal.

Three-dimensional CAD is far more processor intensive than the two-dimensional variety, particularly if the program is designed to give very realistic looking results. This type of thing almost invariably requires a very large screen. Consequently, it is an application where even one of the larger upmarket portable computers could prove to be inadequate. A netbook is likely to be completely useless for 3D CAD work. Unless portability is essential, this is one application where a desktop PC will normally be a much better choice than any portable PC.

Internet

There seems to be a popular misconception that a fairly powerful PC is needed in order to surf the Internet. This is possibly due to the slightly dubious advertising used by some PC manufacturers when the Internet

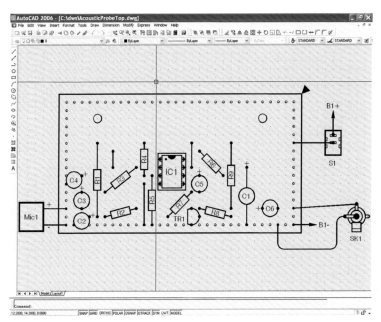

Fig.1.9 A laptop can handle CAD programs, but this is not an ideal task for a netbook

really started to become popular. It was sometimes suggested that a powerful PC would give quicker and more reliable surfing, which is not really the case. In this context the speed and reliability is largely dependent on the speed and quality of the Internet connection. Any netbook PC should be perfectly adequate for surfing the Internet, and is unlikely to be left wanting for speed even when using a fast broadband connection.

It is not even essential to have a large screen in this application. Many Internet sites seem to be optimised for quite low screen resolutions such as 640 by 480 pixels or 800 by 600 pixels. Few require anything beyond 1024 by 860 pixels. Most netbook PCs can handle screen resolutions of this order, although the relatively low vertical resolutions of their widescreen format displays means that a bit more vertical scrolling than normal might be required. The built-in webcam and microphone of many netbook PCs is an obvious advantage for web applications that require these facilities.

Photo editing

The increase in the popularity of digital cameras has resulted in a similar rise in the popularity of photo editing programs such as Photoshop Elements and Paint Shop. Programs of this type mostly require a fairly high screen resolution, which might render then unusable with some computers. A large screen size with high resolution is preferable in this application.

The amount of memory and the processor power required for photo editing depends on the nature of the images that will be processed. Low-resolution images for use on the Internet are not very demanding in either respect. The same is not true of high-resolution images of the type produced by most modern digital cameras. On the face of it, a netbook is of very limited use in this application. However, there are online photo album sites, many of which offer some basic but useful editing facilities, and one of the larger and better specified netbook PCs can work well with one of these.

Multimedia

With desktop PCs there are specials that are primarily designed for use in multimedia applications. There are also fancy media PCs that are designed to blend into the average living room rather better than a typical desktop PC. Last, and by no means least, there are laptop PCs that are primarily designed for multimedia applications, but as far as I am aware, there is no such thing as a media netbook. The fact that netbooks lack any form of built-in CD or DVD drive severely limits their media capabilities. They act as MP3 players, and there will often be a media player program such as Windows Media Player included as standard.

This will probably be capable of playing things such as AVI, DivX, and WMV movie files as well. Watching television "live" or time-shifted using something like the BBC iPlayer, should also be possible. However playing DVDs might not be a practical proposition with a netbook PC, even with the aid of an external DVD drive. The processing required to play DVDs could be beyond the capabilities of the CPU and the graphics system.

Games

Most portable PCs are not well suited to playing computer games. I suppose that their suitability is to some extent dependent on the types of game that you will be playing. Things like Solitaire, old "classic" action games, and puzzles do not usually require a great deal of computing power and high-speed graphics cards. The latest games with high resolution animations of almost photographic quality do require a top-notch graphics card and processor.

Of course, most of the latest action games can be run at lower resolution and with fewer colours, and the demands on the hardware are then much reduced. Unfortunately, they are still likely to be beyond the capabilities of even the highest specified netbook PCs.

If you really must play the latest games while on the move there are a few laptops that have potent processors and fast three-dimensional graphics cards, and these are specifically aimed at those requiring a good games performance from a mobile PC. No doubt these work very well, but so they should as they are very expensive. Large amounts of computing power tend to consume similarly large amounts of power, so a powerful laptop can reasonably be expected to have a very large battery and (or) a short battery life.

Illustration software

The requirements for illustration software and similar graphics programs are quite demanding, and are much the same as those for CAD software. This renders netbook PCs of limited use in this general type of application. In fact the typical hardware of a netbook is inadequate to run most of these programs.

Video editing

Having a very small and portable computer that could be used for video editing when filming on location is a very attractive proposition, but video editing is an application where a netbook PC is unlikely to be usable. Video editing software places huge demands on the computer's hardware, and it tends to generate huge amounts of data. It is an application where a powerful processor, plenty of memory, and a huge hard disc drive are usually considered essential. Digital video is normally transferred via a Firewire interface, which is something that is not normally to be found on a netbook. Video editing on the move therefore requires a well specified laptop or notebook PC, and is unlikely to be possible using a netbook.

Cloud computing

One way of reducing the burden on the computer is to use cloud computing as far as possible. This type of computing is by no means new, but it has dramatically increased in popularity in recent years. In fact, if you use a PC it is virtually certain that you already do a certain amount of cloud computing. Cloud computing is where you use resources that are not located on your computer, or even on a local area network (LAN) to which it is connected. In the current context, the resources will be located on servers anywhere in the world, and in most cases you will have no idea of their location. They are of course, accessed via the Internet.

Probably most users undertake a certain amount of cloud computing without actually realising it. In fact many computer users do substantial amounts of cloud computing practically every day without realising it. Internet based Email systems are a common example of cloud computing. With these systems it is often possible to use an ordinary Email program to access your account, but most people do not bother to do things this way. Instead, they simply use the Email program that is included as part of the system.

The exact way in which things are handled varies from one Email system to another, but you do not normally have an ordinary Windows program running on your PC. At most, some sort of applet will be run on your PC. To some extent the Email program will be running on the server of the service provider, and all your Email data will also be stored on this server rather than on your computer.

This is really just a variation on the system used in some large networks where there is a large and powerful mainframe computer and numerous terminals. Each terminal has very little built-in computing power, and it is basically just sending characters typed into the keyboard to the mainframe computer, perhaps together with information from a pointing device as well. It also receives information from the mainframe computer, and this is used provide the display.

These terminal units are sometimes called "dumb terminals" in order to differentiate them from the type that consists of a PC or some other powerful computer connected to a network. This term is not entirely apt because most terminals are based on a microcontroller, and they do have a certain amount of computing power. However, this computing power is just used to control the flow of data to and from the terminal, and the application software does not run on the terminal. It runs on the mainframe computer, which also stores the data. Cloud computing can operate in a similar fashion with a netbook operating as a "dumb" terminal, and the application software running on the computer at the other end of the Internet connection.

An Internet search engine is perhaps the best example of extreme cloud computing. The user's PC has to do nothing more than send a few words of text to the search engine, and then display the pages of text that come back from it. The search engine does all the work using either a powerful mainframe computer and a huge database, or a huge network of smaller computers. This enables billions of web pages to be searched using massive computing power and database facilities, but the user needs nothing more than the most basic of PCs and an Internet connection.

Similar systems are used for many other online facilities, such as messaging systems, blogging sites, social networking, and online picture albums. With all of these it is a very convenient way of doing things, because the facilities are to a large extent Internet based anyway. In many cases you use your normal web browser to access the facilities, which appear to the user as just an ordinary part of the Internet. There is no need to download and install complex software and then link it to the appropriate Internet site, thus avoiding the complications that this often involves.

It is now possible to take cloud computing beyond facilities that are already web oriented by using the services provided by Google, Microsoft, and others. For example, rather than installing a word processor on your computer and storing your documents on its hard disc drive, you can word process online. You use a program on the provider's server, which is also where you store your documents. Copies of the documents can also be stored on your computer, but this is optional.

Silver lining

There is an obvious advantage in cloud computing for users of netbook PCs. With limited built-in resources it makes sense to utilise, as far as possible, resources located elsewhere. The importance of cloud computing depends on the specification of your netbook. There is clearly a very big advantage when using a minimalist netbook that has no hard drive and has to rely on some form of Flash memory for program and data storage.

The lack of internal storage becomes of far less importance when using programs stored and running on a server, and when the generated data is also stored on the server. A paucity of computing power also becomes less important, since it is a computer at the other end of the Internet connection that is doing most of the hard work. Modern netbooks often have a hard disc of reasonable capacity, and the power of the processor is usually adequate for many applications, but there can still be advantages in cloud computing.

Perhaps most obviously, even where a netbook has a reasonably large hard disc drive, it will still become full over a period of time. Just how long this takes depends on the type of computing involved, and in some cases it could be a matter of months rather than years. The use of cloud computing can greatly reduce the amount of data stored on the hard disc, and help to ensure that the disc never becomes full.

A portable PC such as a netbook is often used in conjunction with a desktop PC or perhaps with a network of PCs at the user's place of work. This brings the problem of synchronisation. Work will be undertaken on some files using the netbook and another computer. When working in the conventional fashion, changes made to a file on one computer will not be applied automatically to the equivalent file on the other computer. It is up to the user to keep the two sets of files up-to-date, preferably without accidentally overwriting any new files with older versions! This process is termed "file synchronisation", but these days it is often just called "synchronisation".

A big advantage of cloud computing is that it enables the problem of synchronisation to be avoided completely. In order to achieve this it is simply a matter of using cloud computing with the netbook and the main PC. You are then working on the same files with both PCs, and synchronisation is clearly irrelevant when there is only one set of data files in use. With cloud computing it is possible to have several people using the same files, and from wherever they can obtain Internet access, making it well suited to collaborative efforts.

An obvious attraction of cloud computing at the moment is that it is largely free. There is the cost of the Internet connection, but this is presumably something that practically every netbook user would have anyway. Some cloud computing services do actually require the user to pay a subscription fee, and this seems to be quite common with online data backup services. Most other types of cloud computing are free though, and are presumably supported by advertising.

It remains to be seen whether most cloud computing services remain free, or a subscription has to be paid. For the foreseeable future it seems likely that increased competition will keep most services free of charge. It also seems likely that there will be a steady increase in the range of cloud computing services on offer.

A big advantage of cloud computing for netbook users is that it makes the lack of a built-in optical drive unimportant. Any software required in order to use online services usually consists of nothing more than a small applet that has to be downloaded. There are no installation discs, and an optical drive is therefore unnecessary.

Drawbacks

Although there is much to be said in favour of cloud computing, it is not a case of "roses all the way". It is by no means a new concept, but it has only recently become popular. Previous attempts to introduce the computers and infrastructure for cloud computing failed before they had even started properly. Interest from potential users was practically non-existent. This contrasts with the current state of affairs where netbooks outsell any other type of computer, and cloud computing is a normal part of computing life.

The main reason for cloud computing having consistently faltered until quite recently is probably a matter of connection speed. Most Internet users had ordinary dial-up connections until a few years ago. These have a maximum connection speed of just 56 kilobits per second, which in practice often turns out to be a speed of about 30 to 40 kilobits per second. Many dial-up users find it difficult to get connected to the Internet in the first place, and reliability thereafter can be poor.

Cloud computing using this type of connection to the main computer system is not a very practical proposition. Everything can run very slowly even when relatively small amounts of data are being swapped between the main computer and the netbook. An unreliable connection will waste more time and make it difficult to use the system effectively. A slow connection is impractical in situations where large amounts of data are being transferred, since the user might have to sit there waiting several minutes for the system to start responding again.

A modern broadband connection is typically about one hundred times faster than a dial-up type. While this is still much slower than an ordinary Ethernet network, it is fast enough to make many types of cloud computing a practical proposition. Probably of equal importance, broadband Internet connections are far more reliable than the dial-up variety. It is inevitable that some users experience problems, but for most people the connection operates reliably for months at a time once it has been installed and set up correctly.

Provided you have a broadband Internet connection, cloud computing is now a practical proposition and it is being used by a rapidly increasing number of people. Unfortunately, it is not really something that can be recommended for anyone who will have to rely on a dial-up connection. An ordinary modem is almost invariably part of the standard specification for a notebook or laptop computer, but it is not usually included as standard with a netbook PC. Obviously an external dial-up modem connected to a USB port can be used if it is essential to use this type of Internet connection, but a broadband connection is needed in order to use cloud computing properly. Netbook PCs usually have an Ethernet port and a wi-fi adaptor included as part of the standard specification.

Another potential drawback with cloud computing is that it is available for many mainstream applications, but for more specialised tasks there will probably be no alternative to conventional software. In practice it is likely that few users will need their netbook for anything other than mainstream applications, but it is something to bear in mind if you are one of the few that will need to use one for niche applications.

Of course, using a mixture of cloud computing for mainstream purposes and ordinary software for more specialised applications is a perfectly valid approach. I would guess that many netbook owners use a mixture of cloud and conventional computing. This is not necessarily because they need to use any niche software on their netbook computer. In many cases it is simply a matter of sometimes preferring to use their favourite conventional software to the cloud alternatives. If the netbook has the wherewithal to use some of your normal application programs, common sense dictates that you should use them unless cloud computing offers some major benefits.

Security issues

As malicious software and hacking are ever present threats on the Internet, security is obviously a concern when using cloud computing. Provided you take the normal safety precautions such as using a firewall and up-to-date antivirus software, there should be a minimal risk of anyone gaining access to your data by hacking into your netbook. There have been cases of large companies having their web sites hacked, but the data stored using online servers is almost certainly more secure than the data stored on your own PCs.

Netbook computers are small, light, and relatively easily to steal, so data stored on your netbook is almost certainly more at risk than data stored on a cloud computing server. Any sensitive information stored on a netbook PC should be encrypted, and ideally there should be nothing of use to thieves stored on any portable computer. On the face of it, cloud computing has the big advantage of avoiding the need to store any data on the computer's hard drive or other internal storage device. Thus, no data is lost and made available to others if the netbook is mislaid or stolen.

Of course, this only applies if the netbook does not have user names and passwords stored on it in some way. Setting up your netbook so that you can enter sites without having to manually type in user names and passwords is a very convenient way of doing things, but it is really not a good idea with any portable PC. It makes it easy for anyone with your computer to gain access to the data you have stored online. Anyway, cloud computing should not be any less secure than the conventional variety, and it could actually be more secure.

It is perhaps worth mentioning that some netbooks have a security slot. This enables the computer to be used in conjunction with a netbook security lock, which is basically just a gadget that is used to tether the computer to any convenient object that is suitably substantial. I do not know whether this method would frustrate a determined thief, but it should be more than adequate to prevent casual theft while your attention is other than on the netbook.

Another aspect of security is how reliably, or otherwise, is your data being stored. Are you going to go online one day and find that your data has disappeared forever? With conventional computing it is normal to make at least one backup copy of any important data. With cloud computing there will usually be no problem in making backup copies of data and storing them on the computer's hard disc drive or some form of external storage such as Flash cards. However, to some extent this defeats the point of cloud computing.

It should not really be necessary to make backup copies of any data produced during cloud computing sessions and stored on the host's server. The server should have an automatic backup system that stores copies of all the files on another server that it situated many miles away from the main one. If the main server goes wrong, is damaged by fire, or runs into any sort of problem, the backup server should be unaffected and your data will be safe.

If you are the type of person who does not bother too much about making backup copies of data, cloud computing actually gives increased reliability since it automatically produces backups for you. Although making backup copies of files is optional, I still do so when dealing with important files. However, the copies are either stored on the hard disc drive of a desktop PC, or on external storage media such as CDs. I do not store them on the internal hard disc drive of the netbook PC.

Operating systems

When you buy a desktop PC it normally comes complete with the latest version of Windows. The situation is much the same with notebook and laptop PCs. Things are very different with netbooks though, where the supplied operating system will not necessarily be the latest version of Windows, or any version of Windows. Instead, it might be supplied with an old version of Windows, a version of Windows designed specifically for small and portable computers, or Linux. The netbook I purchased recently came complete with the Home version of Windows XP, but Windows 7 had just been launched and Vista had been around for a couple of years.

The problem when using the latest version of Windows with a netbook PC is that recent versions of Windows are far more demanding on the computer's resources. Windows Vista requires large amounts of memory and hard disc space in order to run well, and it really needs something a bit more powerful than a typical netbook microprocessor. Older versions of Windows are less demanding and run well on relatively simple hardware. A modern netbook often has a reasonable amount of hard disc capacity and plenty of memory, but the lack of processing power is still likely to be a stumbling block when running Windows Vista. No doubt many netbook PCs are capable of running Windows Vista, but in many cases the level of performance would not be adequate.

Of course, there are drawbacks when using an old operating system, and one of these is that some of the most up-to-date software will not run on older versions of Windows. There can also be difficulties with some peripheral devices due to a lack of suitable driver software. The operating system should not be so out-of-date that this becomes a major problem, and bear in mind that many of the most up-to-date applications require substantial hardware resources in order to run properly. They would not run well, if at all, on a typical netbook computer even if it was running a suitable operating system.

Windows 7 has been designed to provide the advantages of Windows Vista, and more, without requiring the vast hardware resources needed to run Vista effectively. This potentially gives the best of both worlds, providing the netbook user with an up to the minute operating system that supports modern hardware and will run the latest application software. At the time of writing this it is too early to say how successful

Windows 7 will be when used with netbook PCs, but it seems likely that it will soon take over from Windows XP.

Linux

Very few desktop, notebook, or laptop PCs are sold with Linux preinstalled, but it is a very popular operating system in the world of netbooks. I suppose the most obvious advantage of Linux is that it is free, although there are some costs involved when using a version that has proper customer support. Some netbook PCs are offered with Linux or Windows preinstalled, and as one would probably expect, the Linux version is usually significantly cheaper.

Another advantage of Linux is that it will run well on the relatively basic hardware of a typical netbook. There are plenty of versions that have been customised specifically for use on PCs that have a relatively basic hardware specification. Most versions come complete with a range of application software, including office applications, games, graphics applications, media players, and browsers. Like Linux itself, these are usually free. Do not assume that software is of low quality because it is free. Much of the free Linux software is of excellent quality.

Although Linux has points in its favour, there are a few things that have to be borne in mind when deciding whether to opt for Windows or Linux. Linux often comes complete with a Windows style user interface that is fairly easy to ease, but it is not the same as Windows. A certain amount of learning is required when an experienced Windows user changes to a computer running Linux.

Also bear in mind that Windows software will not run on a computer that runs under Linux. If you have Windows software that you will need to run on your new netbook, then you have to opt for Windows. Windows driver software will not operate with Linux either. In order to use internal or external hardware with Linux it is essential to have the correct Linux driver program. Linux has much better hardware support than was once the case, but it is still advisable to check that suitable drivers are available for any peripheral gadgets you will need to use with it.

The free software that is often supplied with Linux, and the other free Linux software that is readily available, is generally considered to be a big advantage of Linux. However, this is not necessarily the case. Netbook users tend to rely on cloud computing to a large extent, with relatively little conventional software installed on the computer. The free software provides no advantage if you will never actually use it.

Also, there is a large amount of free software available for computers that run under Windows. In fact much of the free Open Source Project software that is available for Linux is also produced in Windows versions as well. This includes the very popular OpenOffice business software suite, and the GIMP graphics program. Consequently, it would probably be a mistake to let your decision be swayed by the free software included with Linux.

Getting started

First steps

Traditionally, PCs are supplied in one huge box, but on opening that box you find it contains at least three more fairly large boxes, and probably a selection of smaller ones as well. Fortunately, things are more straightforward with a netbook PC. Having the base unit, monitor, keyboard, and pointing device merged into one small unit helps to keep the clutter to a minimum, which I suppose is the main reason many people opt for a netbook or other portable computer instead of a desktop PC. Of course, the box will almost certainly be much larger than the netbook itself, but the added bulk is largely padding to protect the computer on its long journey from the factory to your front door. The box should also contain at least one or two accessories plus their packaging, which result in further bulk.

Fig.2.1 A netbook PC should be supplied complete with at least one battery

Fig.2.2 The mains adaptor usually acts as the battery charger as well

As a minimum there should be at least one battery and a charger/mains power supply unit (Figure 2.1 and 2.2). There might be one or more CDs or DVDs containing the operating system or a recovery system, and various bundled application and utility software. However, these are not necessarily included with netbook PCs, which have no built-in optical drive, and require an external unit in order to load software from CD or DVD.

The recovery disc will often be in the form of a folder or partition on the hard disc drive that contains the data needed to put the computer back to its factory state. In other words, it takes the hard disc drive back to the state it was in when you first took it out of the box. Any data, programs, or settings added since then are lost. A recovery disc is therefore only used as a last resort when attempts to repair the operating system have been fruitless.

If an operating system or recovery DVD is not included, there will usually be a facility for creating a recovery disc. This will only be usable if an external CD or DVD writer is available, and an external CD or DVD reader will be needed in order to use the recovery disc. Where possible, it is definitely a good idea to make a recovery disc. Having a recovery facility on the hard disc drive provides a quick and easy way to retrieve the situation to get the computer running again when the operating system has been damaged beyond repair. The obvious flaw in this system is that it is unusable if the recovery section of the disc has been corrupted, or the disc drive is faulty and has to be replaced. A recovery disc or an

Fig.2.3 There will probably be one or two thin printed manuals to help get you started

installation disc for the operating system is then needed in order to get the computer operational again.

There might be some leads, such as one to connect the netbook's audio output socket to a hi-fi system. A built-in dial-up modem is not a standard feature of modern netbook computers, but where appropriate there should be a lead to connect the built-in modem to a standard BT telephone socket. There should be a "Getting Started Guide" or something similar, and there might also be a "User Guide" (Figure 2.3), but do not expect much in the way of printed instruction manuals. In most cases there is a more detailed instruction manual or some form of Help system on the hard disc drive. What, if anything, you get beyond that depends on the make and model of PC that you have purchased, and whether you bought any optional accessories.

A desktop PC, unless it is primarily intended for business use, it is almost certain to be supplied with an amplifier and loudspeakers. A netbook

PC is unlikely to be supplied with external loudspeakers as standard, but it will probably have built-in speaker, or even stereo speakers. The small size of the built-in speakers inevitably limits their sound quality though. This makes them far from ideal when using the computer to listen to music.

Carrying a decent set of external loudspeakers around with you is not a practical proposition, but any netbook PC should have a socket for stereo headphones. These should provide much better audio quality than the built-in speakers, and are clearly well suited to mobile operation. A set of headphones might be included with the netbook, but they will probably have to be purchased separately. Any headphones intended for use with portable audio players should work well with a netbook PC.

Modern PCs, netbook or otherwise, are often marketed as systems that contain various peripherals that would once have been very expensive optional extras. These usually offer good value for money and make it relatively easy for a complete beginner to buy and set up a computer system. You are unlikely to get a netbook as part of a huge system, but you still have be careful to avoid buying a system that contain expensive items that you are unlikely to find useful, or simply duplicate equipment that you already own.

Although very popular at one time, docking stations for laptop PCs seem to be something of a minority interest these days. Docking stations for netbooks seem to be virtually nonexistent. This is probably due to the fact that the basic specification of modern computers is much higher, which reduces the need for a unit that gives increased expansion potential. With its "barebones" specification, I suppose a netbook docking station has the potential to be very useful. It is unlikely to be an option though, so peripherals such as USB hubs and optical drives have to be bought individually.

Discarding

It is tempting to throw away the box and other packaging as soon as the computer has been unpacked. This is not necessarily a good idea though. Retailers and manufacturers generally prefer faulty items to be returned complete with all packaging. Apart from other considerations, this helps to keep everything safe during the journey back to the shop or factory. It is particularly important to keep the packaging if the computer has been purchased via mail order. Using the original packing should ensure that the computer remains undamaged if you are unlucky and it should be necessary to return it.

Of course, the packaging is unlikely to be of any further use in cases where the computer is covered by some sort of long term onsite maintenance contract. It should then be safe to discard it all at the earliest opportunity. However, check through all the packing materials very carefully before throwing them away, just in case they contain a small accessory that you have overlooked.

Positioning

With a desktop PC you have to give some thought to the positioning of the computer beforehand, rather than waiting until it arrives. The same thing applies with a netbook if you will be using it a fair amount at home. When using a netbook away from home you generally have to operate it anywhere that provides a reasonable working environment. It is a case of "beggars cannot be choosers", and you just have to put up with things like the odd awkward reflection on the screen, or slightly cramped working conditions.

You have to be more particular when using a PC at home if you will spend a fair amount of time sitting in front of it staring at the screen. It will be difficult to use the computer if the working conditions are mediocre or poor, and you could soon find yourself suffering from various aches, pains, and strains. This is definitely a case of "prevention is better than cure", and it is something that should be taken seriously.

It is not a good idea to position the computer opposite a window. Although monitors have anti-reflective coatings to reduce reflections from the glass screen, no coating approaches complete effectiveness. The coatings on most flat panel monitors are actually quite good, but are perhaps rather less so with the tiny screens used on netbook PCs. With the monitor facing a window it is likely that parts of the screen will be very difficult to read during daylight hours. In fact much of the screen could be impossible to read on really bright days.

Also avoid having the PC itself or any component in the system close to a radiator or heater. Netbook PCs are designed to have low power consumptions, and they consequently generate less heat than desktop PCs, or even laptops and notebooks. On the other hand, they still generate a certain amount of heat, and lack built-in ventilation systems of the type built into desktop PCs. Like desktop PCs, they need to be positioned where they will keep reasonably cool. Feeding them with additional heat is asking for trouble. When the system is installed and operational, never cover or in any way hinder the flow of air through any

*Fig.2.4 Make sure that you have a multi-way mains adaptor if your
netbook will be used with peripheral gadgets*

ventilation grilles. Doing so could easily result in costly damage to the
equipment and could even be dangerous.

Modern netbook PCs often have plenty of black or quite dark plastic on
the exterior, which usually looks very stylish, but does have a practical
drawback. With the sun shining on the computer it can get very hot. As
far as possible, use a laptop PC that has a black or dark case where it is
out of direct sunlight. It is also advisable not to leave one for long periods
in direct sunlight even if it is not in use.

A netbook can be powered from the mains supply via its charger/adaptor
when used at home. This ensures that the battery is always fully charged
when you need to use the computer "on the move". Ideally the computer
system should be positioned reasonably close to a mains outlet. Having
the computer and the monitor combined into a single unit means that
only a single mains outlet is required in order to supply power to both of
them. Of course, further sockets might be needed for major peripheral
devices such as printers and scanners. If extra mains outlets will be
required, you will probably need a four or six-way mains adaptor (Figure
2.4).

Unpack carefully

When you first receive any new gadget there is a temptation to rush in and get it unpacked and operational as quickly as possible. With something as complex as a PC this is definitely not a good idea. It needs to be unpacked and set up carefully. Unpacking the PC itself is unlikely to pose many problems. There are sometimes bits of cardboard that have to be carefully removed from the externally accessible disc drives before they can be used, but a netbook will not have a drive of this type. It might still be necessary with an external CD/DVD drive if you obtain one as an optional extra. The screen of the monitor might be covered by a translucent plastic sheet that has to be removed before it is used. There are often further protective sheets to protect the casing in transit.

The system should be supplied with an instruction manual that gives details of any obscure bits of packing that must be located and removed. These days most computer equipment is supplied complete with a "Getting Started" booklet, "Quick Start" sheet, or whatever, that includes information of this type. Always have at least a quick read through any documentation of this type. A netbook PC is relatively straightforward, so there might not be anything vital in the guide. On the other hand there could be some crucial information, and a quick initial check might avoid unnecessary problems later on. You should certainly read through the "Quick Start Guide" (or whatever) for any major peripheral gadgets supplied as part of the system. It might even prevent you from making an expensive mistake.

If the system includes a printer or scanner it is virtually certain that these will have some odd bits of packing material that must be removed before trying to use the equipment.

Fig.2.5 As supplied, the head of a scanner is often locked

Scanners and printers have moving parts that are usually locked in place during transit. They are often held in place by bits of cardboard, plastic, foam material, and the like. These are often hidden somewhere inside the equipment. Some units, and scanners in particular, have a proper locking mechanism that must be released prior to use (Figure 2.5).

It is very important to carefully read the documentation supplied with the system, and to remove any bits of concealed packing material, undo locking mechanisms, or whatever. An attempt to use the equipment without doing so is likely to result in problems such as chewed-up bits of packing material getting into the mechanism, fuses "blowing", etc. The equipment could easily become damaged, and the guarantee is unlikely to cover this type of thing.

Cover up

Most of the packing material will be pretty obvious, but non-technical people sometimes have problems with the computer's ports and plugs that connect to them. The plugs on computer leads are often supplied with transparent or translucent covers that must be removed before the plugs can be fitted into the connectors on the PCs. Be careful not to overlook the transparent type. Some of these covers look as though they are part of the connector and tend to be easily missed unless you actually look for them.

The ports on the PC are sometimes hidden behind some form of cover. One purpose of these covers is to protect the ports during transit. They can also help to keep dust out of the ports when they are not in use. The simplest type is just a plastic cover that plugs into a port. These are simply pulled free to reveal the port, but it is advisable to leave them in place until the port is required. It is advisable to keep these covers so that they can be put back in place on a port that will not be used for some time.

The more elaborate covers are built into the case of the computer and typically slide to one side and reveal several ports. It is advisable to slide the cover into the closed position when the laptop is on the move. Unless none of the ports are actually used it will probably be necessary to have the cover in the open position the rest of the time.

Checking the contents

Computer manufacturers have checking procedures which should ensure that you receive everything that you have paid for, right down to the smallest of accessories. Mistakes can occur though, so you need to check that there are no missing items as soon as everything has been unpacked. It is now standard practice for a check list to be included in the box, and this should list the netbook itself plus any items of significance that are supplied with it.

It is unlikely that a major item such as a mains charger/adaptor will be omitted, but things such as software discs, leads, adaptors, and documentation do get omitted from time to time. Carefully check that each item listed is actually present, including any seemingly minor items. Some of these might not seem to be of great importance, but you might find that somewhere down the line their absence brings things to a halt. Act at once if you are unlucky and something is missing.

Any large accessories purchased with the laptop will almost certainly have their own box and check list. It will therefore be necessary to do separate checks for any items such as printers and scanners. The check list should include a section that tells how to make a claim for missing items. Legally it is the responsibility of the retailer to supply any missing items. You will usually get the speediest result by taking the system back to the shop if you bought the item locally.

Retailers sometimes suggest that you cut out the middle-man and make a claim direct to the relevant manufacturer. Depending on the nature of the problem, this might be quicker than getting the retailer to sort things out. However, you are under no obligation to do so. The retailer has supplied unsatisfactory goods and it is their responsibility to put things right, but use a little common sense here.

Power

Once everything has been unpacked it is time to start connecting everything together. Computer systems usually have quite a number of cables to connect, which can make things a bit confusing at first. Matters are much easier with a netbook PC because the keyboard, monitor, and pointing device are integrated with the main unit. With a charged battery installed it is possible to use the computer without connecting it to anything.

Probably not for long though, because the battery will soon run flat and will have to be recharged. These days, rechargeable batteries mostly seem to be supplied in an almost discharged state. Therefore, the battery will have to be charged before the computer can be used in earnest. This is something where it is essential to read the instruction manual and follow the manufacturer's recharging procedure precisely. Modern rechargeable batteries are much tougher than those of a few years ago, but there will probably be some guidelines that have to be followed in order to ensure a long operating life. Replacement batteries tend to be quite expensive, so you have to treat them with respect and make them last as long as possible.

You will probably have to install the battery, but it is sometimes supplied already fitted to the computer. In some cases it is not only preinstalled, but is not actually removable by the user. In general, it is better to opt for a netbook where you can replace the battery yourself, and the vast majority of netbooks are of this type. One drawback of a built-in battery is that it will have to be replaced at some stage, and this might not be something that the user can do for themselves. The computer will probably have to be returned to a service centre, which can be costly and time consuming. Also, it is obviously not possible to carry a spare battery for emergency use if there is no quick and easy way of changing the battery.

With some netbook PCs the battery is recharged by removing it from the PC and then fitting it into the charger unit. The latter might also be the computer's mains adaptor, or there could be a separate adaptor. The modern trend is for the battery to be left inside the computer and recharged from a combined charger and mains adaptor. This is again something where it is necessary to read the instruction manual, or perhaps consult the "Quick Start" guide, to determine how battery recharging is accomplished with your particular netbook.

With notebook and laptop PCs it is often the case that recharging the battery takes longer than it does to run it down, or that the charge and discharge times are about the same. Fortunately, the situation is usually different with netbooks due to their much lower power requirements. Many people still opt to recharge the battery overnight, and this should provide more than enough time to fully recharge the battery even if it is completely exhausted to start with. However, it is not really necessary to do things this way since it often takes only an hour or so to fully recharge the battery.

It is possible that the manufacturer will state that the battery is supplied in a fully charged state. In theory, it is then just a matter of installing the battery and using the computer, or simply switching on if the battery is preinstalled. It is unlikely to be as simple as that in practice though. There could have been a gap of weeks or even months between the new laptop leaving the factory and you switching it on. The battery is almost certain to have largely run down during this time. You will then have to recharge it before using the computer, regardless of what the instruction manual may say.

Bear in mind that most rechargeable batteries tend to lose their charge relatively quickly, and do not retain their charge for months and years like alkaline and other non-rechargeable batteries. A new battery should not lose its charge in a few days, but it will probably have to be recharged if the netbook has not been used for a few weeks. Eventually the battery will start to lose its charge quite quickly, or its capacity will become greatly reduced. Fully charging and discharging the battery a few times might cure the problem, but it will probably have to be replaced with a new one.

Any portable PC should have a built-in battery gauge utility that shows the approximate amount of charge left in the battery, and an estimation of the remaining time before the battery becomes fully exhausted. The time quoted can only be estimation, since the actual time depends on the type of work being done. In general, applications that require intensive use of the processor will run down the battery much faster than those that do

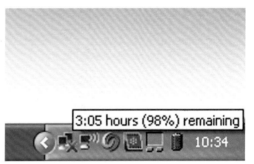

Fig.2.6 The battery gauge shows the amount of charge remaining

not. The battery gauge is usually accessed via the toolbar at the bottom of the Windows desktop (Figure 2.6).

Battery changing

There may never be any need to remove the battery from the computer if you only have one battery, it is preinstalled, and it is charged while in the computer. It will otherwise be necessary to remove and reinstall a battery from time to time. Most netbook batteries are quite large and run virtually the full width of the computer. They are rather like elongated digital camera batteries (refer back to Figure 2.1).

Fig.2.7 The slider on the left is operated first. Operating the slider on the right then enables the battery to be removed

The battery has to be held firmly in place, but it is unlikely that a screwdriver will be needed in order to remove the cover from the battery compartment. There could well be a double catch mechanism though, as in the example of Figure 2.7. The first catch has to be slid to one side before the second one can be operated and the battery can be removed. Note that there is normally no cover to remove from the battery compartment of a netbook. In order to save size and weight, the bottom of the battery also forms part of the netbook's base. Therefore, it is normally just a matter of operating the two sliders and removing the battery. Refer to the instruction manual if there are any problems in removing the battery, and do not try the brute force approach, which would be almost certain to damage something.

Make a note of the battery's orientation before removing it from the compartment. It is highly unlikely that it will be possible to fit the battery the wrong way round, but installing a battery is quicker and easier when you know the correct orientation. With the battery removed (Figure 2.8), the new battery can be installed, and this is usually just a matter of pushing it down into position until you hear a "click" as it locks in place. Try to avoid touching the electrical contacts of the battery or the battery

Fig.2.8 The empty battery compartment, ready for the new battery to be installed

compartment. Doing so can lead to corrosion on the contacts and a poor electrical connection. The current drawn from the battery is quite high, which means that a really good electrical connection between the battery and the computer is essential.

Getting connected

In real world computing it is normally necessary to connect a PC to various external devices, even if it is a netbook type. A netbook has a built-in keyboard and pointing device, but there is a big advantage in using an ordinary mouse whenever possible. Even if you are reasonably expert at using the built-in touch pad or other pointing gadget, using a mouse is still likely to be a far quicker and easier way of controlling the computer. I find the built-in pointing devices of portable computers virtually impossible to use, making a mouse essential. For the home netbook user an external keyboard could also be worthwhile.

Both are offered as optional extras for many netbook PCs, but any normal USB keyboard or mouse should be suitable. A netbook PC does not have the old PS/2 style connectors for a keyboard or mouse, so it is important to obtain USB types. Some PS/2 keyboards and mice are supplied with a USB adaptor, and one of these should be perfectly suitable. It is also possible to buy a PS/2 to USB adaptor, should you wish to use an old PS/2 keyboard or mouse with your netbook PC.

Fig.2.9 Two USB ports. There is a third on the other side of the computer

Fig.2.10 A PS/2 connector

A USB port is a general-purpose type that can be used with a wide variety of peripherals, including large devices such as printers and scanners. Most modern desktop PCs have several of them. Physical constraints mean that there are likely to be fewer USB ports on a netbook PC, but there will probably be at least two of them, and probably more. They will not necessarily be in a single group, and there might be two on one side of the computer and one or two more on the other. In the example of Figure 2.9 there are two USB ports, but there is a third one on the other side of the computer. Separating the USB ports is not necessarily a bad thing, and will often make them easier to use.

It is easy to tell which type of mouse or keyboard you have, since the standard keyboard/mouse connector looks very different to a USB type. The original PC keyboard connector was a large 5-way DIN plug, but this type of connector has not been used with PC keyboards for many years. It has been replaced by a miniature version, as shown in Figure 2.10. The new type of connector is usually called a PS/2 type, as it was first used on IBM's PS/2 range of PCs. The mouse and keyboard connectors are respectively a light green colour and mauve. USB plugs are easily distinguished from PS/2 types because they have a much flatter shape (Figure 2.11).

You need to be aware that some keyboards and mice are of the so-called "wireless" variety. Normally the mouse and keyboard are powered from the PC, but this is clearly not possible if there is no connecting

Fig.2.11 A USB connector is much flatter than the PS/2 variety

cable from the PC to the keyboard or mouse. Wireless peripherals are usually powered by one or two AA or AAA cells. A set of batteries should really be included with the system, but in practice this will not necessarily be the case. The connection from the computer to the keyboard or mouse is provided by an infrared or radio link. Both methods require a receiver that is connected to the appropriate port of the PC, usually via a short cable.

Which USB port?

In general, it does not matter which USB port is used for a given peripheral, since all the USB ports of a PC are usually identical. There are actually two types of USB port, which are the original (USB 1.1) and the new high-speed version (USB 2.0), but the USB specification permits a few variations that can result in a sort of mixture of the two. Ports that conform to the full USB 2.0 specification can be used with any USB devices, including USB 1.1 types. Of course, things work at the old USB 1.1 speed if you use a slow peripheral with a high-speed USB port. With anything like this the system is always limited to the speed of the slowest part of the system.

If you have a PC with USB 1.1 ports, it will work with most USB 2.0 devices, but some will not operate at all without the additional speed of a USB 2.0 port. Other units will work with an old USB port, but more slowly and not necessarily in a worthwhile fashion. Neither a keyboard nor a mouse requires high-speed operation, so both should work perfectly well with any USB port.

Implementing several USB ports that conform to the full USB 2.0 specification presents no problems with a desktop PC, since it has a large power supply that can easily accommodate the relatively high power levels that can be drawn from these ports. It is not really a practical proposition with a netbook PC, where using several power-hungry USB 2.0 devices would run the battery flat in a few minutes, if it could actually supply that much power at all. Consequently, there will be "strings attached" to operation of the USB ports. With (say) three USB ports, there might be two that are restricted to slow devices that have low levels of current consumption, such as mice and keyboards. The third would then be a high-speed type suitable for use with fast peripheral devices such as hard disc drives and optical drives.

Note that any high-speed USB ports might still fall short of the full USB 2.0 specification in terms of the maximum power that can be drawn. A high-speed USB device might need to have its own power source in order to work properly with a netbook PC. It should soon be apparent if you connect a fast USB device to a slow USB port, or if the port cannot supply the power required by the peripheral. Windows should detect the problem and display a suitable warning message.

The computer's instruction manual should detail the capabilities of the USB ports, but in practice the manuals are often very vague in this respect. This does not matter too much if you will only use slow devices that draw little or no power from the port. With other types of USB peripheral it might be necessary to use some trial and error in order to find a USB port that gives the desired result. Wherever possible, USB devices that require relatively high power levels should be powered from their own mains adaptor or battery supply.

It is worth bearing in mind that the Windows operating system might get confused if you do not use the same port each time you use a particular USB device. Windows might consider that the device is a new piece of hardware if you connect it to a different port. The "new" hardware will then be installed by Windows. This does not matter too much, but you can end up with each device installed in Windows several times as several different pieces of hardware. This is not generally considered to be a good idea, and it can certainly make troubleshooting difficult if something goes wrong. While not being essential, it is preferable to always use the same port for each USB peripheral.

Finding the ports

Modern PCs are not exactly short of ports, with a number of them on the rear panel, and probably a few more at the front. Netbooks are generally much less well equipped in this respect, but there should still be plenty of ports scattered around the case. Do not expect the ports to be grouped together in desktop PC fashion. The small size of a netbook means that there is little space available to accommodate the ports. Netbook PC designers do their best to have the ports placed ergonomically, but they are constrained by the practicalities of the situation.

You should soon get used to things, but initially it will probably be necessary to do a little searching to find the ports you need. The actual ports present vary somewhat from one netbook to another. A typical complement would be something along these lines:

USB ports

As already pointed out, these are the computer's main means of communicating with major peripheral devices such as printers and scanners, and they can also be used with things like keyboards and mice. The flat shape of the connectors means that they are easily distinguished from the other types of connector. There should be at least a couple of USB ports, and there should preferably be three or more. The USB ports of a netbook are entirely standard both physically and electronically. You can therefore make the connections to major peripherals using an ordinary (A – B) USB cable.

Smaller peripherals mostly have a built-in USB plug or lead that connects to a netbook's USB ports in the normal fashion. Some small peripherals such as cameras and music players use a miniature USB connector, and therefore require a lead that is fitted with a miniature USB plug. Note that some small USB devices have a non-standard miniature USB connector, and therefore require a non-standard USB lead. A suitable lead is normally supplied with such devices, and it is completely standard at the end which connects to the PC.

"It does not fit" is a common complaint when newcomers to the world of computing try to connect everything together. The computer manufacturers' help lines apparently receive numerous calls from the owners of new PCs who cannot get one item or another connected to the base unit. An important point to bear in mind is that the orientation of plugs is often important. There are exceptions, such as the miniature jack plugs that are often used in computer audio systems, but in most

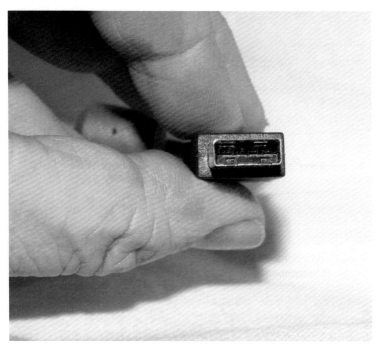

Fig.2.12 A USB plug has one half solid and one half hollow

cases a plug will not fit if it is upside-down, or even if it is rotated a few degrees from the correct orientation. A USB connector certainly has to be fitted the right way up.

The correct orientation often becomes obvious if you look carefully at both connectors. If you look at a USB plug you will see that it has one half solid and the other half hollow (Figure 2.12). The connector on the PC has a complementary arrangement that makes it impossible to fit the plug upside-down (Figure 2.13).

If it is not possible to see the connector on the PC properly, just try the plug one way, and if that fails, try the opposite orientation. The "hammer and tongs" approach is not the right one with electronic equipment, and attempting to force plugs into sockets is likely to damage something. A plug will fit into a socket once the orientation is correct. It will not fit into a socket properly if the orientation is not correct, and shoving a bit harder will not change that fact. It might damage one of the connectors though,

*Fig.2.13 USB ports have a complementary hollow and solid
arrangement*

and this type of thing is unlikely to be covered by the guarantee. New
connectors are notorious for being a bit reluctant to fit together, but some
wiggling and no more than firm pressure is more likely to be successful
than using brute force.

As pointed out previously, there is a potential lack of compatibility between
the USB ports of a netbook and some USB peripheral devices. A USB
port can supply power to a peripheral gadget, but the amount of power
that could reasonably be drawn from a netbook PC is quite low.
Consequently, a netbook could be unable to operate with some USB
gadgets that draw their power from the PC. There should be no problem
with low power devices such as keyboards and mice, or with devices
that are specifically designed for use with portable PCs. The latter will
either be designed to have a suitably low level of power consumption, or
will be self-powered. It is best to only use major USB gadgets that have
their own power source. It is probably scanners that lack their own power
source that are most likely to give problems. Again, as pointed out
previously, an error message to that effect will normally be produced on
the screen if a USB device tries to draw too much power from the port,
so the nub of the problem will be pretty obvious.

There is a way around this problem in the form of a powered USB hub.
The basic function of a USB hub is to enable several peripheral gadgets

*Fig.2.14 A modem port. This is for a dial-up connection and not a
broadband type*

to be used with a single USB port on a computer. A powered hub includes
a power supply that enables the hub to provide the full quota of power to
each of its USB ports with no power being drawn from the computer.

Modem port (Figure 2.14)

Some laptop and notebook PCs have a built-in modem, but it seems to
be a rarity with netbooks. Where a modem is included, it is a standard
56k dial-up type and not one for use with any type of broadband Internet
connection. Its absence on most netbooks is perhaps a pity, since there
could be situations where you have access to an ordinary telephone
socket, but no form of broadband connection is available. The port
connector on a netbook is usually a miniature telephone type and not a
BT telephone connector. Leads to connect this type of port to a UK
telephone socket are readily available from computer stores, but a suitable
lead will almost certainly be supplied with the computer.

Note that there is a small lever on the plug that connects to this port
(Figure 2.15). This is part of a locking mechanism that operates

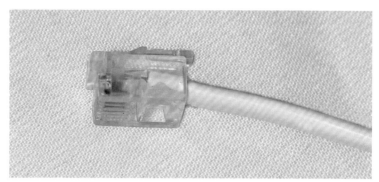

Fig.2.15 The plug on a modem lead has a lever that unlocks it from the modem port

automatically when the plug is inserted into the modem socket. The lever must be pressed in order to release the plug so that it can be removed from the socket. Forgetting to press the lever before pulling the plug free is a common way of damaging these plugs, which are mostly of rather lightweight plastic construction.

Fig.2.16 An RJ-45 Ethernet port

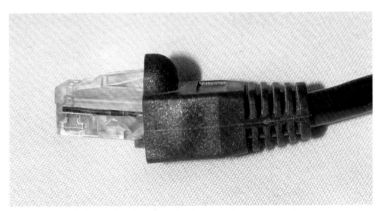

Fig.2.17 An RJ-45 plug is a locking type with a release lever

RJ-45/Ethernet Port (Figure 2.16)

An Ethernet port is sometimes referred to as a RJ-45 port, which I think is a reference to the type of connector used. Anyway, this interface enables the netbook to be connected to a standard PC network. It is also used for some types of broadband Internet connection. RJ-45 connecting cables use the same type of connector at each end, and can be connected either way around. There are two main types of RJ-45 cable, which are the straight and crossover varieties. Straight cables are used for most networking connections. The crossover type is used when two computers are directly linked via their Ethernet ports, rather than being connected via some form of router.

Like modem plugs, the Ethernet variety have a lever (Figure 2.17) that must be operated before the plug can be disconnected from the socket. Although Ethernet and modem connectors look similar, they are in fact totally different and incompatible. The Ethernet connectors are significantly larger than the modem variety.

Video (Figure 2.18)

Although a netbook PC has a built-in monitor, it seems to be standard practice for a video output socket to be included. This is usually a standard 15-pin (HD15) analogue type that is compatible with any normal PC monitor. The more expensive flat panel monitors also have a digital input that can be used with a DVI video output (Figure 2.19). This type of video connector is becoming more common on desktop PCs and will

Fig.2.18 Many laptops have a standard 15-pin video output

probably replace the HD15 type in due course. It is still a rarity on netbook PCs, but will probably take over from the HD15 in the coming years.

Fig.2.19 Few laptop or netbook PCs have a DVI video connector

Fig.2.20 4-pin (left) and two 6-pin (right) Firewire ports

In theory anyway, the digital video signal of a DVI interface can provide better picture quality than the analogue signal of a HD15 interface. Consequently, where the computer and the monitor both have a DVI interface, these should be used to provide the link between the two units. In practice there is usually no obvious difference in the picture provided by the two types of interface.

Firewire/IEEE 1394 (Figure 2.20)

Firewire, which is also known as an IEEE 1394, is a high speed serial port that was originally designed to accommodate the high data rates associated with high quality digital video. It is still in widespread use with digital video cameras and other digital video equipment. In the past it was mainly associated with Mac computers, where it was effectively the Mac equivalent of the USB ports on PCs. Many PCs are now equipped with Firewire ports as standard, or have them available as an optional extra. Firewire is now used as a general purpose port, and it is not restricted to digital video applications.

Firewire ports are only included as standard on some of the more upmarket laptop and notebook PCs, but seem to be a rarity on netbooks. In fact they do not seem to feature on any current netbooks. Neither is there any way of adding one, such as using an expansion card. Consequently, it will be necessary to opt for a suitably equipped laptop

Fig.2.21 The power port. Only use the correct mains adaptor

or notebook if you really must have a portable PC that is equipped with this type of interface.

Power port (Figure 2.21)

A netbook PC would in some ways be neater and easier to use if the mains power supply unit was integrated with the main unit. Possibly some netbooks do indeed have integrated power supplies, but I have not encountered one of this type. Messing around with external power supplies seems to have become an essential part of modern life, and every household seems to accumulate a fair number of them. I have a drawer containing more than a dozen, and there are several more scattered around the house.

With many types of equipment an external adaptor is the only realistic way of handling things. The small size of a netbook would make it difficult, but probably not impossible to integrate the power supply with the main unit. However, this would mean carrying the extra weight of the power supply around with you even if you did not intend to power the computer from the mains supply or recharge the battery. An external power supply is cumbersome and a drawback when using a netbook as a home computer, but only a minor one.

Fig.2.22 The audio output socket is primarily intended for use with headphones

A fair amount of electronic equipment is damaged each year by people accidentally using the wrong adaptor. In the likely event that you have a number of these units, make sure that you always use your laptop with the right one. There are probably protection circuits in all laptop PCs, but it is still possible that using the wrong mains adaptor could result in a lot of expensive damage.

Legacy ports

These are ports that were once used as the main means for a PC to communicate with peripheral gadgets such as modems and printers. However, these days there are more modern ports available for this type of thing, such as the USB and Firewire types. Consequently, these older ports are now little used and will ultimately be phased-out altogether. They are not included on netbook computers.

There is obviously a problem if you have an old peripheral with a serial or parallel port that you wish to use with your laptop PC. Wherever possible it is probably best to replace the peripheral with a modern device that has a USB port. There is a potential solution in cases where it is not practical to replace the peripheral gadget. It is possible to obtain adaptors that enable serial or parallel devices to be used via a USB port (refer back to Figure 1.4 in Chapter 1). These do not work well in all situations, but in most cases a unit of this type will permit the peripheral to be used with your netbook PC.

Fig.2.23 The audio input socket will normally work with a microphone

Bear in mind that getting an old gadget connected successfully to a PC and actually getting the computer to work with the gadget are two different things. There are several potential problems, but the main one is that the old gadget will only work with a new PC if there is suitable driver software available. Driver software for older versions of Windows is usually of no use with the current versions. Most manufacturers of PC peripherals do not produce modern drivers for use with older equipment that they consider to be obsolete.

Audio output (Figure 2.22)

This is one respect that a netbook PC is likely to be much more straightforward than a desktop type. The latter usually has at least three audio sockets, and these days there can be half a dozen or more. A netbook PC is unlikely to have more than three audio sockets, and many have just two. As a minimum there will be an output and an input. The output is likely to be optimised for the types of headphone often used with portable audio devices such as MP3 players, but it should work satisfactorily if connected to active loudspeakers of the type normally used with PCs. Results will probably be acceptable if the audio output is connected to a hi-fi system.

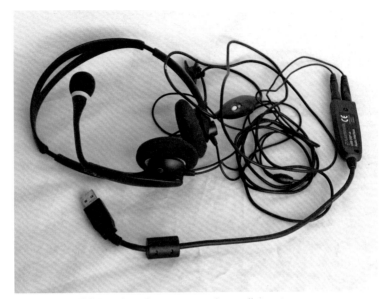

Fig.2.24 A USB headset does not use the audio ports

Audio input (Figure 2.23)

Any netbook should have audio input and output connectors, and the input socket is most likely to be a microphone input. PC microphone inputs tend to be a bit problematic. One reason for this is simply that there are several types of microphone in common use, and an input that is suitable for one type will not necessarily work properly with other types. Another problem is that the original SoundBlaster microphone input was a mono type that included a supply output to power an old-fashioned carbon microphone (as used in old telephone handsets).

Some modern sound systems still have this type of microphone input, although these days it would be used with a modern electret microphone. Some modern PC sound systems have a stereo microphone input and no supply output. These are suitable for dynamic microphones, or for electret types that have a built-in battery. Finding out which type of microphone will work with a given PC is usually a matter of trying the "suck it and see" method.

Fortunately, this is academic for most netbook users. There is usually a built-in microphone and a webcam situated on the lid of the netbook,

Fig.2.25 A Flash memory card slot fitted with an SD card

just above the screen. The quality of the microphone might fall short of hi-fi quality, but it should be adequate for most purposes. While it is not exactly a standard item of equipment, some netbooks are supplied with a headset that includes a microphone, or it is available as an optional extra. Either way, it will presumably be fully compatible with the microphone input of the netbook.

Note that some of the more upmarket headsets do not connect to the audio connectors at all. Instead, they connect to the PC via a USB port. Headsets of this type (Figure 2.24) often have some integral digital processing that is intended to give better results in critical applications such as speech recognition. A big advantage of a USB headset is that it avoids the microphone compatibility problems mentioned previously, and should guarantee high quality results. I have always found a USB headset to be well worth the additional cost.

Flash card slot (Figure 2.25)

A built-in Flash memory card reader is now quite common on practically every type of PC, with Flash cards having largely taken over from floppy discs. An integral Flash card reader is more or less a standard feature on netbooks. Although these devices are normally referred to as "readers", this name is a bit misleading. As far as I am aware, all Flash card readers make it possible to write data to the cards as well as reading it.

One slight problem with Flash cards is that there are several types in common use, and a few more that are less popular or verging on obsolescence. Desktop PCs often include multi-card readers that can handle practically any type of Flash card, but due to space considerations the built-in readers of netbooks tend to be less accommodating. The practical consequence of this is that it will be necessary for you to use the type of card that the netbook will accept, rather than expecting the netbook to use whatever type of Flash card you normally use.

The nearest thing to a standard Flash card is the SD (Secure Digital) type, which is small enough to be used in tiny portable devices, but is also available with high capacities. Actually, normal SD cards have a maximum capacity of 2 gigabytes, but the high capacity SDHC type is available with much higher capacities. The Flash card reader of a netbook should be able to use either type of SD card, and it might also be able to accommodate two or three other types, such as XD, two types of Memory Stick, and MultiMediaCards (MMC).

Compact Flash (CF) cards are very popular, but the built-in card reader of a netbook PC cannot usually handle this type of card. Although Compact Flash cards are relatively large, in absolute terms they are still quite small and are physically much tougher than most other types of Flash memory card. For this reason, they are preferred by some users to the lighter but more flimsy cards, such as SD and XD types. Of course, there is no real problem if it is essential to use a Compact Flash card with a netbook PC, and it is just a matter of using a suitable external card reader plugged into a USB port of the computer (Figure 2.26).

There are sometimes limits on the capacities of the cards that can be used, and the computer's instruction manual should give details if there are any "strings attached" to the built-in card reader. It only takes a small amount of dust in a card slot to prevent it from working properly, so the slot will sometimes have a sliding cover that should be kept closed when it is not in use. Alternatively, there might be a dummy card that can be used to protect the slot when it is not in use.

A small memory card as used with netbook computers is removed by momentarily pressing it in slightly. It will then spring out a little from the slot so that it can be pulled free. A card is installed in the slot by simply pushing it into place until it locks into place. The card must be the right way up, and it will not fit far into the slot if it is the wrong way up. Trying to force memory cards into place when they are the wrong way up is a popular way of damaging the cards and the main hardware. Never try to force a card into place, even if it is the right way up. There is

Fig.2.26 A separate card reader will probably be needed for CF cards

something amiss if it will not slide easily into place, such as the card being slightly damaged, or some dust in the slot.

The Flash card reader will be treated by the operating system as a removable disc, like a floppy disc drive. It is important that it has this status, since the operating system would otherwise be confused if the Flash card was removed and replaced by a different one. The operating system will detect the change each time you remove a card and insert a different one into the card reader, and it will then adjust to the contents of the new card. This should ensure error-free operation.

Card speed

The read and write speeds of Flash memory cards was not of great importance in the days when a large card was one that had a capacity of about 16 or 32 megabytes. It started to become a major issue when card capacities started to go above the one gigabyte level. Large cards now have a capacity of 16 or 32 gigabytes rather than megabytes, which is about one thousand times greater than the capacities of the early Flash cards. Reading the contents of a slow 32 gigabyte could literally take all day!

The "Flash" name tends to give the impression that this type of memory is extremely fast. Unfortunately, the name refers to the process used when writing data to the card, and it is not meant to imply super-fast operation. The reading and writing speeds of Flash memory are actually quite slow by current standards, and they are not even very fast when compared to various types of true disc storage. Most Flash memory manufacturers use a speed rating that is essentially the same as the one used for CD-ROM drives. There is a slight difference in that the rating used for a CD-ROM drive is the maximum it can achieve, and the actual speed obtained near the middle of the disc is usually much lower. There is no Flash memory equivalent to this, and the quoted speed should be obtained when writing to any part of the disc.

A speed rating of X1 is equivalent to about 150 kilobytes per second. Most memory cards are not actually marked with a speed rating, although this information is usually included in the manufacturer's data. A card that has no marked rating usually has a speed of about X4 to X12, and can read or write data at about one megabyte or so per second. Note that there is no point in using a faster card with a reader that has a USB 1.1 interface, or is connected to a USB 1.1 port. A "bog standard" memory card can transfer data at a rate that is about double that of a single device on a USB 1.1 port.

At the time of writing this it is possible to obtain memory cards that have speed ratings of up to about X266, although it seems likely that significantly faster cards will be developed. These cards are mainly intended for use with electronic gadgets that handle large amounts of data, such as digital video cameras and the more upmarket digital cameras. However, they also offer the potential for moving large amounts of data from one PC to another in a reasonably short time, or for backing up data.

A card having a rating of X60 for example, can read and write data at up to nine megabytes per second. In theory at any rate, a gigabyte of data could be written to the card in less than two minutes. Cards having speeds of around X133 are now available at quite reasonable prices, and these can read or write a gigabyte of data in under a minute. SD cards are often stated to be class 2, 4, or 6, and the class number is the guaranteed minimum transfer rate of the card in megabytes per second.

Fig.2.27 A pen drive is useful for transferring data from one PC to another, and for back-up purposes

These correspond to speeds of approximately X13, X26, and X40 respectively.

Flash cards provide an easy way of getting data loaded into a netbook from another PC, and they are also very useful as backup drives. Ideally, a PC should have two hard disc drives so that all the data on the main drive can be backed up on the second drive. The cost of hard disc drives is now so low that this is common practice with desktop PCs, but with a portable PC it is not usually possible to have more than one internal hard disc drive. An external drive connected to a USB port can provide a good alternative, and cloud computing offers another.

Something like a fast 16 or 32 gigabyte Flash card provides another alternative. Slower cards are cheaper, and will probably be adequate where relatively small files and amounts of data are involved, but it is otherwise worth paying extra for something like an X133 or X200 card. Where the hard disc drive is of limited capacity, it is often worthwhile buying a large and fast Flash card and leaving it in the card reader on a semi-permanent basis. It will probably have to be removed from time to time so that (say) picture files from a camera can be transferred to the hard disc drive, but the card can otherwise be left in place and used as a second hard disc drive.

Pen drives

Pen drives are another useful form of external storage for netbook computers. A pen drive is a gadget that looks rather like a short but stubby pen, but removing the top reveals a USB connector (Figure 2.27).

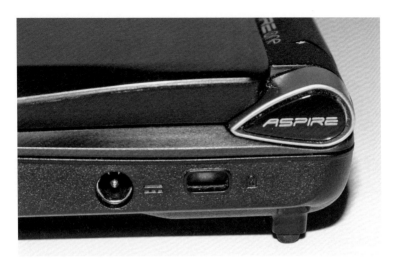

*Fig.2.28 The socket to the right of the power connector is actually a
Kensington security slot*

It is just a USB card reader and some Flash memory in a single unit.
When a pen drive is plugged into the computer it will be added to the
end of the existing series of drive letters. For example, if the PC already
has drives from A to F, the newly added pen drive will be drive G. Windows
usually refers to Flash drive as a "Removable Disk", which is not strictly
accurate since the Flash memory is not removable and cannot be
replaced with different memory. However, this status ensures that
removing the drive will not have dire consequences for the smooth
operation of the PC.

Note though, that it might be necessary to switch off the drive via software
control before it is removed. In fact this will almost certainly be necessary.
There is otherwise a risk of an error message being produced, and the
operating system could become confused. The deactivation process
usually requires little more than operating a button in the Windows taskbar.
The instructions provided with the drive should explain how to switch
the drive on and off.

Security lock

As mentioned in Chapter 1, many netbook computers have provision for
a security lock. This is a mechanical device that enables the netbook to
be tethered to any convenient object that is suitably large and heavy. At

Fig.2.29 The user normally has to complete the final stages of installing the operating system. Here a user name and optional password are entered

first glance the socket for the security lock looks like an electrical connector of some kind (Figure 2.28), but closer inspection shows that there are no electrical contacts.

If you intend to use this feature it is important to obtain a security lock that matches the particular type of security slot on your computer. The Kensington security lock, or "K-slot" as it is sometimes called, is by far the most popular type, but there are alternatives in use. It is therefore important to check this point in the computer's instruction manual before buying a security lock.

The big moment

With a charged battery installed in the computer or a mains adaptor connected to the power port, you are ready to switch on and boot into the operating system. If there are any peripheral devices connected to the computer it is probably as well to do one final check to ensure that everything is plugged in correctly. Are all the plugs fully pushed into their ports on the netbook and making reliable connections? Even experienced computer professionals have been known to spend quite

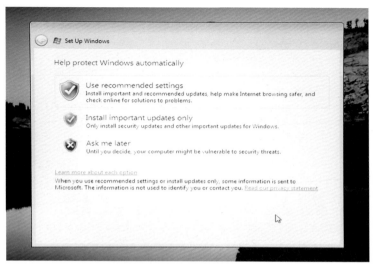

Fig.2.30 This screen provides options relating to automatic updates

some time troubleshooting a new PC before they realise that it is not receiving any power. If you are using the mains adaptor, is it plugged into the mains and is the mains outlet switched on?

The system of on/off switching used for laptops is exactly the same as the one normally used with desktop PCs. Switching the computer on is accomplished by operating a pushbutton switch, which is often to be found on the keyboard near the function keys. It is not usually too difficult to spot, but if in doubt its position should be indicated in the relevant sections of the instruction manual and the Quick Start Guide. The computer is switched off via the operating system, and the Start button in the case of one that is running Windows.

These days computers are supplied with the operating system preinstalled, and there will usually be some bundled software as well. Therefore, when you switch on the computer it will go through the usual start-up and boot routine and go into Windows. Unfortunately, the first time you boot into Windows it is likely that there will be a certain amount of setting up to do, but this is usually just a matter of answering a few simple questions (Figures 2.29 and 2.30). The operating system is not quite fully installed, and you have to go through the final stages of installation before the computer is ready for use.

The exact routine varies depending on the make and model of computer, and the software that is bundled with it. Consequently, it is only possible to give some general guidance here rather than precise information. The documentation supplied with the computer should give all the guidance you will need, and there is often an information sheet that goes through the setting up procedure on a screen by screen basis.

Getting Windows running is not usually the main problem. Many new PCs, whether they are desktop or laptop types, are supplied with some preinstalled application software. Some of this software is will probably be fully functioning, and will prove to be very useful. For example, a full version of the ever-popular Microsoft Works office suite is often bundled with new PCs, and no doubt it is found to be extremely useful by many users. Few, if any, would object to having this type of software preinstalled on their PC.

Some other types of software are more contentious. This is something that depends on the make of computer that you buy, but it now seems to be the norm for various trial programs to be preinstalled on new PCs. These are programs that are limited in some way, or "crippled" programs as they are often termed.

A program of this type will typically work in every respect but with inoperative Help and printing facilities. Another ploy is to have a program that runs normally for (say) 30 days after you first run it, but then refuses to run at all. In a similar vein, many PCs seem to be supplied with preinstalled security suites that can be kept up to date without charge, but only for a few weeks or months. The normal subscription fees then apply. Yet another ploy is for the software to be fully functioning, but in order to use it you must agree to have the pop-up advertising that is included as part of the deal.

The main objection to the bundled trial software is that it can make it difficult to get the computer set up and ready for use. You would like to get into the Windows operating system and start computing, but you find that the bundled software tries to get you to go through all sorts of setting up and registering processes. There may be no way of totally bypassing these processes, and it could be necessary to take a certain amount of time going through the setting up procedures. Understandably, this gets many users more than a little narked!

It is worth bearing in mind that the computer manufacturer is paid fees for including this type of bundled software on their PCs. In effect, the cost of your new PC is being subsidised slightly by the producers of the bundled software. Another point to keep in mind is that no manufacturer will preinstall any form of spyware, adware, or anything that hides on your hard disc drive and cannot be easily removed. Any bundled software can be removed if you do not need it. The correct methods of removing unwanted software are covered later in this book.

Therefore, you can simply go through any unavoidable setting up procedures, and then remove the offending software if it is genuinely of no interest to you. It is not actually essential to remove bundled software that you will not use. Removing unwanted software has the advantage of freeing some hard disc space, although the amount that is liberated will not necessarily be that worthwhile.

There is a slight risk that removing software, even if it is done correctly, will mess up the operating system. This is far rarer than it was in the past, with modern versions of Windows being rather more robust than those of yesteryear. Also, the applications programs and their uninstall programs are more reliable and less likely to damage the operating system.

Windows has a facility know as System Restore which can take the computer back to its previous state if something goes wrong when uninstalling software. There is no guarantee that System Restore will always be able to live up to its name, but it further reduces the risk. However, there is still a slight risk of software removal causing a problem that cannot be fixed easily. Those who are not confident at using Windows facilities such as System Restore might prefer to take the safe option of leaving the unwanted software in place.

You will probably not consider this to be an option if a program keeps producing pop-up messages to the effect that you need to renew your subscription, register it, or something of this nature. It might be possible to go into the offending program and disable the messages via an Options or Preferences window, but this is not always possible. Another possibility is to alter the Windows start-up settings so that the program cannot run automatically, but it is probably easier and safer to simply uninstall it.

Problems

Modern electronics is generally very reliable, but faults can occur and you might be unlucky. A modern computer is so complex that it is probably that bit more likely to go wrong than something more basic such as an MP3 player or a radio. Although a netbook is relatively simple by computer standards, it is still an extremely complex piece of hardware.

Anyway, before taking up the matter with the retailer it is a good idea to check that the problem is not due to a minor problem or mistake that can be easily solved.

If the laptop is doing nothing at all, is it actually getting any power? Where the unit is being powered from the mains adaptor, is the latter plugged in properly, is the mains supply switched on, and is the adaptor plugged into the computer properly? The mains adaptors used with netbook computers sometimes have an indicator light. Does this switch on when the adaptor is plugged into a mains outlet? Multi-way mains boards can be a bit temperamental. If you are using one of these to provide additional outlets, trying using a different mains socket on the panel or plug the adaptor straight into the wall socket.

There is probably a fault in the computer or the adaptor if power is definitely getting through to the adaptor and then to the computer, but the computer fails to respond properly. Computer help lines tend to receive large numbers of calls from customers who have been unable to switch on their desktop computers. They press the button on the front as per the instruction manual, but nothing happens. The problem is that they have failed to realise that there is a conventional on/off switch at the back of the computer, and that it is set to the "off" position. It is unusual for a portable computer to have a conventional on/off switch, but it would be as well to check this point in the instruction manual. It might save some embarrassment later on!

If the computer is being run from a mains adaptor, try powering it from the battery instead. It is likely that the mains adaptor is faulty if the computer can be powered from the battery but not the adaptor. Similarly, it is likely that the battery is a dud or is not being charged correctly if it is possible to power the computer from the mains adaptor but not the battery. Did the battery go through the recharging procedure correctly, with the indicator lights switching on and off at the right times, or whatever? It can sometimes take a few attempts to get a new battery to go through the charging process properly.

It is possible that a little investigation will find the problem and that there will be a simple solution. If not, there is no point in spending large amounts of time searching for the cause of the problem. You must contact the retailer at once if it proves to be impossible to get the computer to power-up and boot correctly after looking for any obvious problems. It is the responsibility of the retailer to sort out any genuine faults, and not yours.

Testing

Assuming the computer will boot into Windows, you should then try to give everything a quick test. For example, will the Flash card adaptor read and write using the appropriate types of card? Does the sound system work correctly, do any peripherals such as a keyboard and mouse function correctly, and so on? If you can find a way of testing any part of the computer, then do so.

If there are any faults, then you need to find them and get them rectified as soon as possible. You should certainly try to avoid the situation where you do not use (say) a port until you have had the computer for some time. If you then find that it does not work properly it is possible that the computer will be out of warranty, and you will have to pay for the repair or get by without the faulty port. Any problem found might be of the hardware variety, and very obviously of the hardware variety. For example, a problem such as a keyboard where one or more of the keys tend to jam is obviously a mechanical fault. It is then a matter of returning the faulty item to the retailer.

In other cases the cause of the problem might conceivably be in software, such as a faulty driver program or an incorrect setting in Windows. For example, a lack of audio is almost certain to be caused by a software problem such as an incorrect setting in Windows, a faulty driver program, or a media player program that is not set up correctly. Odd problems with the display becoming corrupted are usually due to a faulty driver program rather than a hardware problem. However, if the display is fine with the computer's lid at some angles, but not at others, there is clearly a mechanical/electrical problem.

The retailer will probably have a help line of some sort, and they might be able to provide an easy fix for the problem. If you are having problems with a faulty set-up, then it is likely that everyone else that has bought that make and model of PC will be having the same problem. With anything like this the retailer or manufacturer should soon come up with a solution which should then be available from any relevant help lines.

Note that some of these help lines are not free, or have "strings attached" such as only being free for a limited period. You should not really have to pay for information that helps to get a faulty product working properly. If a computer fails to work properly you are not obliged to use an expensive help line. You can, for example, take it back to the shop and get them to fix the problem.

Where the computer is covered by an onsite maintenance contract you should be able to invoke the contract and get someone to fix the problem at your premises, and free of charge. Many computer manufacturers and the larger retailers have web sites with a support section, and this will usually have details of any common problems and suitable fixes. There might be some sort of technical support available via Email. Anyway, it is certainly worthwhile checking the retailer's or manufacturer's web site for support services.

Turn off

It is not unknown for Windows to boot up correctly, but to give problems when you try to switch off the computer. Sometimes you end up going around in circles and never actually manage to shut down Windows. The more common alternative is that Windows starts to go through its closing down procedure, and it normally gets close to the end, but at some point it stalls and the computer is not switched off. This problem is less common with Windows XP, Vista and 7 than it was with some earlier versions of Windows, but it can still happen.

The instruction manual for your computer should include details of how to switch it off if none of the normal methods work. This often involves holding down the On button for a few seconds. Directly switching off the hardware is not usually to be recommended, since it tends to leave a number of temporary files on the hard disc drive. These files are deleted by the operating system when the computer is switched off in the normal way. However, Windows XP, Vista and 7 are less easily fazed by these files than some of their predecessors, and Windows should sort things out when it is next booted, as should Linux in a similar situation.

If no other way of shutting down a computer can be found, it must be cut off from its power source or sources. In the case of a netbook this means disconnecting it from the mains adaptor and removing the battery. However, this should be used only a last resort, and the computer should be shut down by other means wherever possible.

There are several possible causes of Windows failing to shut down properly, but these days it is mainly associated with faulty driver software or other programs. Anyway, if this problem occurs before you start installing any of your own software, the problem is almost certainly due to drivers or other software supplied with the computer. Presumably other users of the same make and model of computer will be experiencing the same problem, and the manufacturer should quickly come up with a solution. The relevant customer support service should be able to supply you with details of this solution.

Fig.2.31 The free version of AVG offers a useful range of features

Antivirus software

A netbook is often used in conjunction with the Internet, and might only be used for applications that require an Internet connection. It is therefore crucial to have up-to-date security software installed on a netbook. Any modern version of Windows will come complete with a basic Firewall program, and there will often be an additional Firewall in the router/modem that provides the Internet connection. These should be sufficient to keep all but the most determined hackers at bay.

It is also important to have antivirus software that is equipped with an up-to-date virus database. These days every new PC seems to be supplied with a preinstalled antivirus program, but the virus database will only be updated for a limited period. This is typically about one month, and after that the program will either cease to work at all, or it will continue using an out-of-date virus database. Either way, your netbook will be left vulnerable to attack by viruses and other malicious software.

One solution is to simply renew the subscription to the preinstalled antivirus software. This is fine if the software works well and you are prepared to meet the costs involved. If you decide not to renew the subscription, it is not a good idea to go on using the out-of-date database or to simple carry on without any form of antivirus protection. There are some good free antivirus programs that also have no ongoing costs involved. Regular updates to the virus database are free of charge. AVG Free (http://free.avg.com/gb-en/homepage) is probably the best known of these, but there are others. Do not assume that free antivirus software is inferior to the normal subscription variety. The free programs such as AVG Free (Figure 2.31) usually perform very creditably when pitted against other antivirus programs in tests by computing magazines and others. They are certainly a vast improvement on using no antivirus software at all.

Removing programs

As pointed out previously, it is likely that the new computer will have been supplied with some preinstalled software that is of no interest to you, and which might actually be a bit of a nuisance. Removing unwanted software from a PC is not usually too difficult, but it is important to go about things in the right fashion. Simply deleting the files and folders associated with programs you wish to remove is definitely going about things in the wrong fashion. It will certainly free some hard disc space, but deleting program files and folders is also likely to produce a few problems.

Most programs are installed onto the computer using an installation program, and this program does not simply make folders on the hard disc and copy files into them from the CD-ROM. It will also make changes to the Windows configuration files so that the program is properly integrated with the operating system. If you simply delete the program's directory structure to get rid of it, Windows will not be aware that the program has been removed. During the boot-up process the operating system will probably look for files associated with the deleted program, and will produce error messages when it fails to find them.

Matters are actually more involved than this, and there is another potential problem in that Windows utilizes shared files. This is where one file, such as a DLL type, is shared by two or more programs. In deleting a program and the other files in its directory structure you could also be deleting files needed by other programs. This could prevent other programs from working properly, or even from starting up at all.

If a program is loaded onto the hard disc using an installation program, the only safe way of removing it is to use an uninstaller program. There are three possible ways of handling this.

Custom uninstaller

Some programs load an uninstaller program onto the hard disc as part of the installation process. This program is then available via the Start menu if you choose All Programs, and then the folder with the name of the program concerned. If there is no folder icon for the program, just the normal entry that is used to launch it, then that program does not have an uninstaller or other additional software available.

Fig.2.32 An uninstall option is available in this example

Even if there is a folder icon for the program, it is possible that there will be no uninstall option available there. The example of Figure 2.32 shows the submenu for the AVG Antivirus program, and this one does include an option to uninstall the program. Uninstaller programs are almost invariably automatic in operation, so you have to do little more than instruct a program of this type to go ahead with the removal of the program.

With any uninstaller software you may be asked if certain files should be removed. This mostly occurs where the program finds shared files that no longer appear to be shared. In days gone by it did not seem to matter whether you opted to remove or leave these files. Either way, Windows usually failed to work properly thereafter! These days things seem to be more reliable, and it is reasonably safe to accept either option. To leave the files in place is certainly the safest option, but it also results in files and possibly folders being left on the disc unnecessarily.

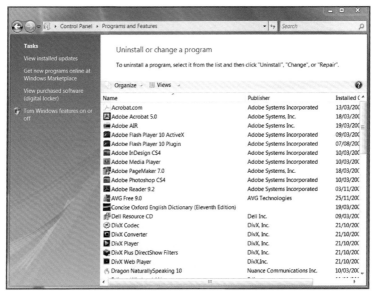

Fig.2.33 A list of all the installed software is provided

Windows uninstaller

Windows has a built-in uninstaller that can be accessed via the Windows Control Panel, which can be launched from the Start menu with any modern version of Windows. The exact route to the uninstaller depends on the version of Windows in use, and whether you use the normal or "Classic" version of the Control Panel. It is probably best to resort to the Windows Help system if there are any problems finding the uninstaller. Using "uninstall" as the search string should produces pages that have links to the uninstaller.

The exact appearance of the uninstaller depends on the version of Windows in use, and the software installed on the computer, but the main section of the screen always shows a list of the programs that can be uninstalled via this route (Figure 2.33). Removing a program is basically just a matter of selecting it from the list by left-clicking its entry, and then operating the Uninstall/Change button. Changes to the system, including the removal of programs, will normally require you to confirm that you do actually wish to make the changes. This is a security measure designed to prevent hackers or rogue programs from making malicious

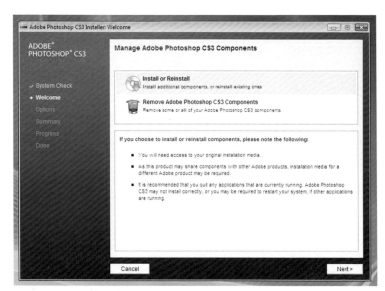

Fig.2.34 The program can be installed, reinstalled, or removed

alterations to the system. Operate the Continue button in order to carry on with the removal of the program.

The next step depends on the particular software that you are removing, and it may simply be necessary to confirm that you wish to remove the selected program. In many cases, and particularly in the case of major pieces of software, there will be more than one course of action open to you. In the example of Figure 2.34 there is a choice of installing or reinstalling the software, or removing it. In the current context, it is clearly the option of removing the program that is selected. The other option is used when it is necessary to install optional extras that were not chosen when the software was originally installed, or where a program has become corrupted and is not functioning correctly.

In theory, the list of removable programs should include all programs that have been added to the hard disc using an installation program. In practice there may be one or two that have not been installed "by the book" and cannot be removed using this method. Some programs can only be removed using their own uninstaller program, while others have no means of removal at all. It is mainly older software that falls into the non-removable category, particularly programs that were written for

Windows 3.1 and not one of the 32-bit versions of Windows. In fact it is very unusual for old Windows 3.1 software to have any means of removal. Fortunately, there is very little software of this vintage that is still in use.

These days it is more likely that there will be programs listed that you do not recognise. It is possible that one or more of these are pieces of malicious software that should be removed, but in most cases they are small programs that are installed with large programs. It seems to be increasingly common for substantial programs to be accompanied by one or more small utility programs that provide additional features. Software of this type should only be removed if you are sure that it does not provide a useful function.

Third party

There are uninstaller programs available that can be used to monitor an installation and then uninstall the software at some later time. As this feature is built into any modern version of Windows, and the vast majority of applications programs now either utilize this built-in facility or have their own uninstaller software, these programs are perhaps less useful than they once were.

Most will also assist in the removal of programs that they have not been used to install, and this is perhaps the more useful role. Most will also help with the removal of things like unwanted entries in the Start menu and act as general cleanup software, although Windows itself provides means of clearing some of this software debris.

Leftovers

Having removed a program by whatever means, you will often find that there are still some files and folders associated with the program remaining on the hard disc. In some cases the remaining files are simply data or configuration files that have been generated while you were trying out or setting up the program. There should obviously be nothing of any importance here when deleting unused software from a new computer. Accordingly, there should be no problems if these files are deleted using Windows Explorer. In other cases the files could be system files that the uninstaller has decided not to remove in case they are needed by other applications. Removing files of this type is more risky and it is probably better to leave them in place.

Unfortunately, it is not uncommon for uninstallers to leave large numbers of files on the hard disc. The uninstaller seems to go through its routine in standard fashion, and reports that the program has been fully removed, but an inspection of the hard disc reveals that a vast directory structure remains. I have encountered uninstallers that have left more than 50 megabytes of files on the disc, removing only about 10% of those initially installed.

Other uninstallers report that some files and folders could not be removed, and that they must be dealt with manually. Some uninstallers seem to concentrate on extricating the program from the operating system by removing references to the program in the Windows Registry, etc., rather than trying to remove all trace of it from the hard disc.

If you are simply trying to remove a troublesome program that produces annoying pop-up messages, uninstalling it should have the desired result and prevent the messages from appearing. If you are trying to free hard disc space, an uninstaller that leaves many megabytes of files in place is not very helpful. Try to keep things in perspective though. The hard disc drives used in modern netbooks generally have lower capacities than those used in desktop PCs, but the actual capacity is still likely to be quite high at around 160 gigabytes or more. Will removing (say) 100 megabytes (0.1 gigabytes) of files really make that much difference?

Removing leftover files is a bit risky, so due care needs to be taken if you do decide to go ahead. A safe way of handling things is to leave the directory structure and files intact, but change some file or folder names. If only a few files have been left behind, try adding a letter at the front of each filename. For example, a file called "drawprog.dll" could be renamed "zdrawprog.dll". This will prevent Windows from finding the file if it should be needed for some reason, but it is an easy matter for you to correct things by removing the "z" from the filename if problems occur.

If there are numerous files in a complex directory structure to deal with it is not practical to rename all the individual files. Instead, the name of the highest folder in the directory structure should be renamed. This should make it impossible for Windows to find the file unless it does a complete search of the hard disc, and the change is easily reversed if problems should occur. Provided the computer runs for at least a few days with no problems it should then be safe to go ahead and remove the files and folders.

A file or folder can be renamed by right-clicking its entry in Windows Explorer and selecting Rename from the pop-up menu. The name of the file or folder can then be edited in normal Windows fashion. Left-

Fig.2.35 Installing some software requires an external DVD drive

click any blank area of the Window once the necessary changes have been made.

Installing software

Installing software on a netbook can be problematic due to the lack of a built-in optical drive. Most conventional software is supplied on CD-ROMs, but in the case of large programs or suites it is sometimes supplied on DVDs. Where possible, it is probably best to abandon the conventional approach altogether, and opt for cloud computing, or programs that can be downloaded from the Internet such as the Open Source types. These do not require an optical drive for installation, and thus avoid the problem.

Probably most netbook users will wish to use at least one or two of their normal application programs on their netbook PC. One way around the installation problem is to use an external CD-ROM drive or some form of DVD drive connected to a USB port. An external CD-ROM drive can be obtained quite cheaply, and is adequate for installing most software. However, an external DVD drive (Figure 2.35) will obviously be needed if any of the software you wish to install is supplied on DVDs. It is unlikely that a netbook will be able to power any type of optical drive from its USB ports, so it is important to obtain a drive that has its own power source. This is usually in the form of a mains adaptor, but a few drives have a built-in rechargeable battery. Installing software using an external drive is exactly the same as using an internal type.

There are possible ways of installing software from a CD-ROM or a DVD without connecting the netbook to an external optical drive. A netbook normally has an Ethernet networking port, and can therefore be connected to a home or business network without too much difficulty. In theory, a shared optical drive on the network can then be used to install software on the netbook. In practice this method tends to be problematic, but it is worth trying. Software manufacturers often provide installation notes in a text file on one of the supplied discs, and this will usually include advice on installing the software over a network.

Another method is to use a desktop PC to temporarily copy the installation disc to a medium that the netbook can access. This might infringe the licensing conditions of the software, but it is unlikely that a software manufacturer will object to this method of installation provided the copy is deleted as soon as installation has been completed, and the software is otherwise used in a fully legitimate fashion.

The PC is used to copy the contents of the installation disc to either a pen drive or a Flash card that is compatible with the netbook's card reader. This is just a matter of using Windows Explorer and the standard Copy and Paste features of Windows. Obviously the capacity of the pen drive or Flash card must be large enough to take all the files and folders on the installation disc. The maximum capacity of a CD-ROM is about 700 megabytes, and that of a DVD is around 4.7 gigabytes. Modern Flash cards and pen drives with capacities of 8 and 16 gigabytes are readily available, so there is no real problem here.

With luck, it will be possible to install the software from the Flash card in the normal way. Depending on the quality of the card, it might take somewhat longer than normal, but in other respects everything will follow along the normal lines. It will not work if the original installation disc uses some form of copy protection that prevents the software from being installed from anything other than an original disc. There is then no option other than using an external optical drive to install the software.

User accounts

Although "PC" in a computer context stands for "personal computer", I think it is fair to say that most desktop PCs are actually used by several

Fig.2.36 Left-click the link for "Manage another account"

members of the family, or by several colleagues at work, as appropriate. On the other hand, portable computers in general, and netbooks in particular, tend to live up to the "personal" part of the PC name, and are often used by just one person. A practical consequence of this is that user accounts will often be of little importance when using a netbook.

At least one user account will be produced as part of the final installation process for the operating system. This is all that will be needed if the netbook will only be used by one person. It is not essential to generate additional accounts even in cases where other people will regularly use the computer, but it is generally better if each user has their own account. Having separate accounts for each user enables a degree of individual personalisation of the operating system.

Initially there will be one or two user accounts, and where there are two there will be one for the user and an Administrator account. The alternative is to have an account for the user that is also an administrator account. A separate administrator account is usually reserved for making changes to the system or troubleshooting, since it gives full control over the system. The standard user account is then used for normal day-to-day computing. A user account that has administrator status is used for everything, but it

Fig.2.37 Left-click the "Create a new account" link

has to be used with care so that unwanted changes to the system are avoided. Inadvertent changes are unlikely to occur in practice, since Windows tends to provide at least one warning message before any changes can be made to the system.

New account

The exact method used to produce a new account depends on the version of Windows in use, but the first step is to go to the Control Panel where there should be a User Accounts section and (or) an "Add or remove user accounts" link. Once into the User Accounts window you should have something like the one shown in Figure 2.36. Start by left-clicking the link for "Manage another account", and then in the new version of the window (Figure 2.37) left-click the "Create a new account" link. The first task will probably be to type a name for the account into a textbox. As with anything like this, try to use a meaningful name such as the nickname of the person who will use the account. Moving on to the next step switches the window to the one shown in Figure 2.38.

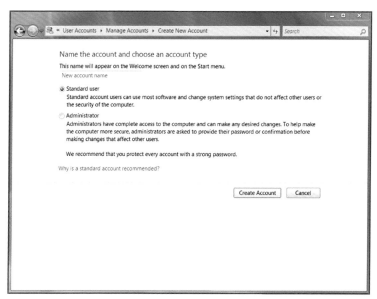

Fig.2.38 Use a meaningful name for the new account

The two radio buttons are used to select the required type of account. As pointed out previously, an administrator account provides freedom to make changes to the system, but these abilities are not needed for day to day use of the computer. A standard account is generally considered to be the better choice for normal use, since the restrictions reduce the risk of the system being accidentally damaged. Note that using a standard account it is still possible to make changes that will not affect the way in which others use the computer.

There are a few additional points to bear in mind if you opt for a standard account. You might not be able to install programs when using this type of account. Any that you do install might not be fully available to other users. Also, some programs produced prior to Windows 2000 and XP might not be usable with a limited account. As already pointed out, it is possible to make changes to the system that will only affect the standard account, but any wider ranging changes, however trivial, are likely to be blocked. It might not be possible to undertake something as basic as uninstalling a program or deleting files when using this type of account. Consequently, there is no alternative to an administrator account if maximum flexibility is required.

Fig.2.39 This window is used to enter the password

Having selected the type of account using the radio buttons, operate the Create Account button. The original User Accounts window then returns, but it should now contain the newly created account. There are other facilities in the User Accounts window that enable the login and logoff settings to be altered. By default, the Welcome screen is shown at start-up, and you simply have to left-click the entry for the new account in order to use it. Note that the new account will start with a largely blank desktop. Each account has its own desktop and other settings, so each account can be customised with the best settings for its particular user.

Accounts are not password protected by default. To add a password, go to the window of Figure 2.36 and left-click the "Create a password for your account" link. At the next window (Figure 2.39) the password is typed into the top two textboxes, and a hint is entered into the other textbox. The hint is something that will jog your memory if you should happen to forget the password. Next operate the Create Password button, which moves things on to a window where the text beneath the account's icon should confirm that it is now password protected. This completes the process, and the password will be needed the next time you login to that account.

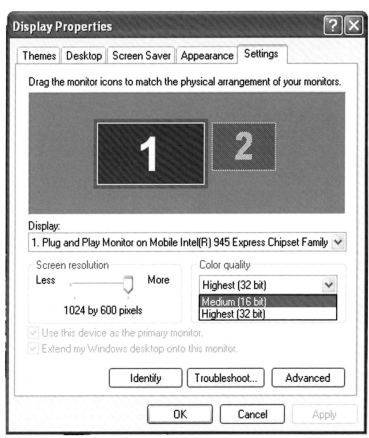

Fig.2.40 Reducing the colour depth can produce an increase in speed

Screen settings

With any new computer it is often necessary to alter the resolution and colour depth settings of the screen. They often default to relatively low settings, and must be set manually to more usable figures. However, the default settings with a netbook will often be the optimum ones. The default screen resolution will be rather low by the standards of desktop PCs, or even the more upmarket laptop and notebook types, but it will probably represent the maximum that the built-in monitor can handle!

It can still be worth checking that everything is as it should be, and the easy way to access the screen settings with Windows XP is to right-click any unused part of the Windows desktop and then select Properties from the pop-up menu. Then select the Settings tab in the new window that appears. With Windows Vista and 7 it is again a matter of right-clicking an unused area of the Windows desktop, but the Personalise option is selected from the pop-up menu, and then the Display Settings link in the new window is activated.

In both cases you should end up with a window that looks something like Figure 2.40. The display resolution is set using the slider control, and this should be set at the maximum resolution of the built-in monitor if it is not already at the appropriate setting. It can be advantageous to use relatively low screen resolution with a PC that has a slow processor. Doing so can result in the computer running noticeably faster. Netbook PCs have slow processors due to the need for minimal levels of power consumption in order to obtain good battery life. However, the maximum resolution of the built-in monitor will not be very high, and using a lower screen resolution could make the computer virtually unusable in some applications.

Another ploy for obtaining speedier performance is to reduce the colour depth setting. In other words, things can be speeded up by reducing the maximum number of colours used by the display generator chip. The default colour depth setting is often for 32-bit operation, which enables many millions of colours to be produced. There is often the option of using 16-bit operation, which gives a palette of more than 65000 colours. With the small screen of a netbook PC this reduced colour depth is unlikely to produce a very noticeable reduction in quality even when viewing colour photographs. In fact there may be no apparent reduction in quality, but a worthwhile increase in speed could be obtained.

Recovery

In the past it was normal for computers to be supplied with a disc containing a copy of the operating system, and some are still supplied with a Windows installation disc. Should any major damage occur to the operating system, making it impossible to boot up the computer properly or rendering Windows unusable for some other reason, with the aid of the Windows installation disc it is possible to reinstall the operating system. This is a rather drastic solution, but there might be no other option in cases where the operating system has become severely corrupted.

Many modern PCs are not supplied complete with a standard Windows installation disc. Instead, they are usually supplied with a recovery disc or discs that can be used to take the computer back to its original state, as supplied from the factory. In some cases the recovery disc is actually a partition or fielder on the hard disc drive. The obvious drawback of this system is that any corruption of the hard disc could damage the recovery "disc" as well as the Windows installation. Some PCs therefore come complete with a utility program that enables a recovery disc or set of recovery discs to be produced.

Although many regard any form of recovery disc as second best to an ordinary Windows installation disc, this is perhaps not entirely fair. Being realistic about matters, if the operating system becomes so badly damaged that the computer will not run or even boot properly, a recovery disc provides a more convenient option than the normal installation discs. The operating system and any bundled software can be quickly reinstalled and you can then try again at getting everything set up correctly.

The exact method used varies from one manufacturer to another, but in general the recovery discs are very easy to use. It is just a matter of booting from the first recovery disc instead of the hard disc drive, and then following a few simple on-screen instructions. However, you need to carefully read through the documentation for the recovery disc before getting started, since some preliminary setting up might be required before they can be used.

Bear in mind that any recovery system that takes things "back to square one" will usually result in the loss of any data on the hard disc drive. This will probably be of no practical consequence when you are dealing with a problem that occurred when initially setting up the computer. It is likely that there will be no data stored on the computer at this stage, or that any you have installed will already be fully backed up. However, where appropriate you must make a backup copy of data stored on the PC before using the recovery discs.

There is an obvious problem when using recovery discs with a netbook PC, which is simply that there is no built-in optical drive for use with the discs. Therefore, in order to use a recovery disc it will be necessary to connect a suitable external drive to the computer. It is quite common for portable PCs to be supplied without a recovery disc, but there is usually the option of using the supplied utility program to produce one (Figure 2.41).

Obviously a facility of this type will only be of use if a suitable optical drive is available. A DVD writer is the best type, since the high capacity

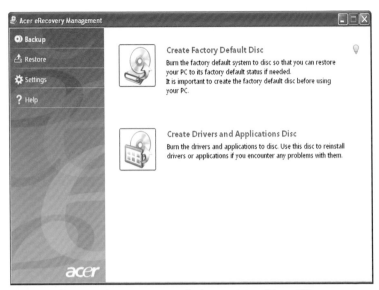

Fig.2.41   Many netbooks are supplied complete with a utility program for making recovery discs

of a DVD will often make it possible to have just one recovery disc, or perhaps one disc for the operating system and another for the preinstalled software.   There will usually be the option of using a CD writer, but with this type of drive the recovery disc could actually be a set of more than a dozen discs.   Unfortunately, it is unlikely that there will be an option to make a recovery disc using a Flash memory card of suitably high capacity, although some netbook PCs have been supplied with recovery discs in this form.

Anyway, where possible it is advisable to make a recovery disc or set of discs if they are not supplied with the computer as standard.   At some future date it might otherwise be necessary to return the netbook to a service centre to have the operating system reinstalled, which could be expensive.   The alternative is to buy the full retail version of the operating system, which would again be quite expensive.

Cloud computing

Browser

The concept of cloud computing was introduced in Chapter 1, and we will not go over the same ground again here. In order to use cloud computing it is necessary to have some form of Internet connection, and preferably a fairly fast type, together with a browser program. It is not necessary to have a special browser for cloud computing, but that is not to say that any web browser can be used with any cloud computing facilities. Most cloud computing services are fairly easy going, and will work with the majority of modern browser programs.

However, it is advisable to check the requirements before trying to using any cloud computing services. Most of them will work perfectly well with the popular browsers such as Internet Explorer and Firefox, but it is as well to ensure that you are using a suitable program, and an appropriate version of that program. If you normally use one of the less popular browsers it is definitely a good idea to check that it is compatible with any cloud computing services that you intend to use.

If problems occur even when using a suitable browser program, it is likely that one or more of the so-called browser plug-in programs are required in addition to the basic browser software. For example, it is sometimes necessary to have something like the Adobe Flash Player add-on installed. Most cloud computing services have a Help section that provides details of any add-on software that is needed, together with installation instructions. Browser add-ons are usually available as free downloads incidentally, so there should be no cost involved unless you have to pay for the Internet access while downloading the file. The typical file size is only a megabyte or two, so the download time should be extremely short.

The lack of a required add-on will often be detected by the facility you are trying to use, and automatic installation may then be offered. These

Fig.3.1 The Google Docs sign-in page

automatic systems do not always operate flawlessly, but they are generally worth a try. Bear in mind that each of the popular web browser programs usually has its own version of the add-on software. If you are using the Linux operating system, check that the facilities you intend to use are compatible with this system.

Remember that it is not necessary to use the same web browser for everything. If your normal web browser is not compatible with a cloud computing facility that you are eager to use, there is an easy solution. Simply install a web browser that is compatible with this facility, and then use it when you wish to use that facility. Your normal web browser can still be used for all other Internet related tasks. Provided your netbook has a reasonably amount of memory installed, there should be no problems if two different web browser programs are run simultaneously.

I think it is worth making the point that the relatively low screen resolution of a netbook PC makes it important not to waste screen space with anything that is optional and unnecessary. Most netbooks have widescreen monitors, which produces a vertical screen resolution which is often quite limited. With any program it can therefore be useful to switch off any menu bars, status bars, or toolbars that are not really necessary.

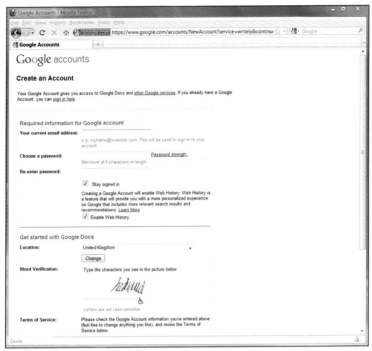

Fig.3.2 Opening a Google Docs account is very straightforward

It is especially important with a browser, since these programs tend to start with several of these bars, and often gain a few more if any add-ons are installed. When a browser is used with web based facilities it is likely that more of these bars will appear, with the extra ones being part of the web based software you are using rather than elements of the browser. Switching off bars that are not really needed, even temporarily, can free some useful screen space and make the web based facility much easier to use.

Word processing

Obviously it is not essential to use cloud computing when you need to do word processing on your netbook, even though it does have some advantages. Windows comes complete with a very basic word processor called WordPad, which is adequate for simple note-taking. Most modern

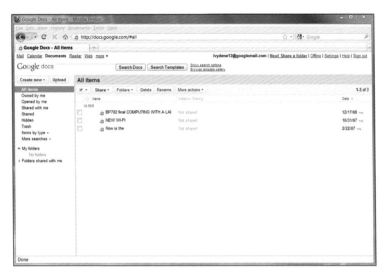

Fig.3.3 The initial Google Docs screen, with three existing documents listed

netbooks are quite capable of running office suites such as Microsoft's Office and the free OpenOffice business software suite if you need something more sophisticated. These run and are used in much the same way whether they are used on a netbook or a powerful desktop PC.

Here we will assume that you wish to try cloud computing, including the cloud version of word processing. Google Docs is probably the most popular cloud computing word processor, and in order to use it you must have an account with Google. A Google account provides access to a wide range of cloud computing facilities including Email, blogging and web site creation. Having a Google account and using Google's cloud computing facilities is something that every netbook computer user should give serious consideration.

Google Docs is actually a bit more than a word processor, since it also includes a spreadsheet facility and a slideshow creator. Go to this web address to make a start with Google Docs:

http://docs.google.com

This will take you to the login page (Figure 3.1), and it is obviously just a matter of signing in if you already have a Google account. If not, operate the Get Started button and enter the necessary information on the new web page that appears (Figure 3.2). Since the Google facilities will be used on a portable computer it is probably best not to use the "Stay signed in" option. Operate the "I accept Create my account" button once the form has been completed.

You can then sign into Google Docs, and the screen will then look something like Figure 3.3. I have already added three documents, which are listed in the main panel on the right. In order to open an existing document it is just a matter of left-clicking its entry in the list, and it will then be opened in a new tab. However, this panel will obviously be blank when starting from scratch, and a new document has to be created by operating the Create new button and selecting the

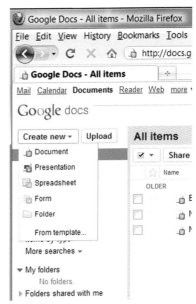

Fig.3.4 Select the Document option from the menu

Document option from the drop-down menu (Figure 3.4). This will produce a blank document in a new tab (Figure 3.5).

The usual facilities of a basic word processor are available when working on a document. If there is a menu bar near the top of the screen, as in Figure 3.5, this is the menu bar of the web browser, and not the one for the Google Docs word processor. This menu bar is situated in the conventional place, just above the main document area. It has the usual menus such as File, Edit, and Format. When you start using Google Docs it is easy to keep going to the wrong menu bar from force of habit, so it might be a good idea to switch off the browser's menu bar.

A point to bear in mind when saving documents is that they are not saved on the hard disc drive of your netbook, but are instead being stored on a Google server. They can be loaded into Google Docs and edited using any computer that has Internet access. If you require hard copies of documents, they can be printed in the normal way using the Print option in the File menu. At some stage you might need to download a document to your computer, so that it can be used with a desktop publishing program perhaps.

Fig.3.5 A blank document has been created, and it is ready for content to be added

One way of doing this is to use the normal Copy and Paste facilities in the Google Docs Edit menu. With some browsers this will produce a warning message which explains that the Cut, Copy and Paste facilities are not available from within Google Docs with the particular web browser in use. However, these facilities can still be used via the equivalent facilities in the browser's Edit menu, or using the normal Windows keyboard shortcuts. Of course, the same facilities can also be used if you need to import text into a Google Docs document.

The alternative is to download the document using the Download As option in the file menu. This has a submenu (Figure 3.6) which offers various file formats that provide compatibility with a wide range of application programs. There are the general Text and rich text formats (RTF), an HTML option, Word and OpenOffice word processor formats, and even the option of downloading the document in Abobe PDF format. When you use the Download As facility you will get the browser's normal pop-up window for handling downloads. This will usually offer the options of saving the file to disc or opening it in the default program for the selected file format. In Figure 3.7 I have opted to download the file in PDF format and open it in Adobe Reader.

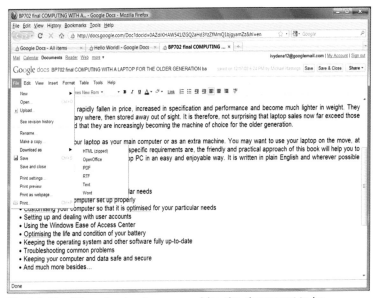

Fig.3.6 The "Download as" menu enables the document to be
downloaded in a choice of several formats

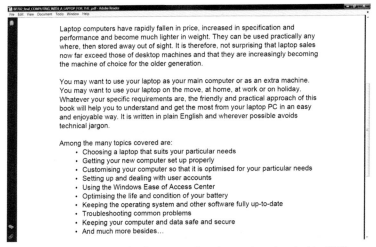

Fig.3.7 Here the example document has been downloaded in PDF
format and is being displayed in the Adobe Reader program

Fig.3.8   The Email company's home page should have a sign-up link, as in this example which shows the Yahoo! home page

Email

Web-based Email and messaging systems are already familiar to a high percentage of computer users, and have become increasingly popular in recent years. Why do so many people use web-based Email systems such as Yahoo and Hotmail when it is normal to be supplied with several Email addresses when an account is opened with an Internet service provider? I think the most likely reason is that the Email addresses provided by your Internet service provider (ISP) are dependent on the account remaining open. If you switch to a different ISP, as most people tend to do from time-to-time, the Email addresses effectively cease to exist and can no longer be accessed.

This is not a problem with an Internet based Email system such as Yahoo or Hotmail, where your Email addresses are not quite immortal, but could well outlive you. Even if you change your ISP annually, your web based Email account will carry on as normal, and can be used whenever you have access to the Internet. The contents of your Emails should be equally secure whether you use an account with your ISP or one with an established web Email service.

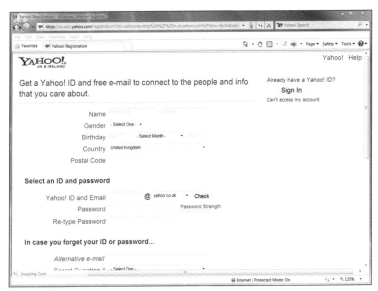

Fig.3.9   Some personal information has to be entered on the sign-up page

When choosing an Email service provider it is advisable to choose one that is likely to remain in business for many years to come, which in practice probably means choosing one of the large and well established services such as those provided by Yahoo!, Microsoft and Google. These larger companies often include other services as part of the deal, but they are optional and you can use only the Email service if that is all you require. These services are all free incidentally, and it seems likely that they will remain so into the foreseeable future.

Signing up to an Email service is usually very straightforward. The home page of the company will usually have a "Sign-up" link displayed fairly prominently, and in the example of Figure 3.8 it is in the top right-hand section of the Yahoo! Home page. It will usually be necessary to provide a certain amount of personal information on the sign-up page (Figure 3.9), but there should be nothing too intrusive. You are usually free to choose the part of the Email address that appears to the left of the "@" sign, so there is plenty of scope to choose something eminently suitable. Unfortunately, with a well established Email company there will be many millions of existing Email addresses, and this can make it difficult to find something suitable. Rather than (say) "bobpenfold@" it might be necessary to settle for something more like "bobpenfold345@".

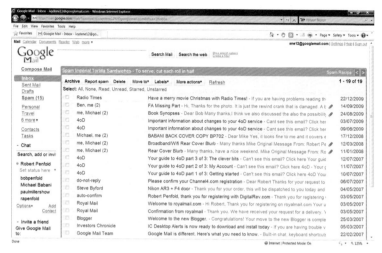

Fig.3.10 A "Classic" layout is well suited to use with a netbook

Classic Email

There is sometimes a choice of Email software, with one option offering a very basic screen layout and another one providing a more complex layout that is similar to that of a conventional Email program such as Microsoft's Outlook Express. The more simple system is usually described as the "Classic" option, and it will usually have a screen layout something like the Google Gmail example of Figure 3.10.

The left-hand section of the screen includes links to the available folders, while the right-hand section lists the Emails within the selected folder. There will usually be too many Emails to list on a single page, but it is easy to scroll through the pages using the arrowhead buttons, and there should be a facility that enables a specified page to be selected. In order to display a page it is merely necessary to double-click its entry in the list, and the Email will then appear in the main panel (Figure 3.11).

Although "Classic" Email systems are perhaps a little rudimentary when compared to the more modern types, they are generally the more practical proposition for netbook users. The screens of netbook PCs have relatively low resolutions, and the use of wide-screen monitors often results in a vertical resolution that is very low by modern standards. If you try to use something other than the "Classic" system it is likely that a warning

Fig.3.11 Double-clicking an entry results in the corresponding Email being displayed

message will appear, pointing out that the software could be difficult to use due to the limited screen resolution. It is unlikely that you will be blocked from using the "de luxe" system, but switching to it could be pointless.

The alternative screen layout is usually similar to the "Classic" type, with the left-hand panel again having a list of available folders. However, the right-hand panel is split in two with, with the upper section showing a list of Emails in the selected folder. The lower section is used to display the selected Email, and it is merely necessary to left-click an Email's entry in order to select it.

This layout does not actually work that well with high-resolution wide-screens, as in the example of Figure 3.12. This is the modern version of the Yahoo! Email system, and the relatively low height of the screen does not provide a great deal of room to display the list of Emails, or the selected Email. It is possible to drag the dividing line between the two panels, but making more room for one of them obviously gives less space for the other one.

Figure 3.13 shows the Yahoo! System in operation with a netbook that has a screen resolution of 1024 by 600 pixels, which is about the maximum that is used with netbooks. It is just about usable, but the "Classic" layout is much more usable, and is the one recommended by Yahoo! for this screen resolution. Double-clicking an entry results in the

Fig.3.12   The standard screen layout does not really work all that well
with a high resolution widescreen monitor

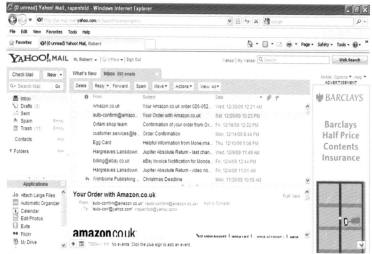

Fig.3.13   The standard screen layout works even less well with a small
widescreen monitor

Fig.3.14   The usual text editing facilities are available when composing a new Email

corresponding Email being displayed in the entire right-hand panel which improves usability, but is really just taking things back to the "Classic" method!

Composing

Whichever Email program you select, there will be the usual facilities for composing, deleting, and moving Emails. A basic text editor will be obtained when a new Email is composed (Figure 3.14), and this will provide the usual facilities for using different fonts, text sizes, and colours. There will also be the standard formatting facilities for text alignment, bold, underline, and Italic styles, and so on. Bear in mind that any formatting will only appear when the recipient views the Email if their Email software is set up to handle HTML. The formatting will otherwise be stripped off and they will see a basic text message.

There is also a facility for sending attachments. There used to be quite low restrictions on the number and size of attachments, but matters have improved greatly in recent years. With modern web based Email systems it is usually possible to have several attachments with a total file size of many megabytes. The amount of storage space for your Emails also used to be quite limited, with a paid-for account being required if more

Fig.3.15 The Google search system has found two Emails that contain the specified key word

storage was required. Again though, things have improved in recent years, and the larger Email companies now include at least a few gigabytes of storage as standard with their free Email services. Apart from spam or other rubbish Emails, most users will not need to delete anything.

Searching

There is a potential problem if you opt to keep every valid Email, and this is simply that you will eventually have a huge number of Emails stored in the system. This can make it difficult to find the one you need, especially if it was sent or received months or years ago. There is usually a Search facility that can be used to hunt through all the stored Emails and search for a key word or several words. These systems operate in the standard search engine fashion.

The example of Figure 3.15 shows the Google system in operation, and it has successfully located the two Emails that contain the specified word. As in this case, there will usually be two versions of the Search facility,

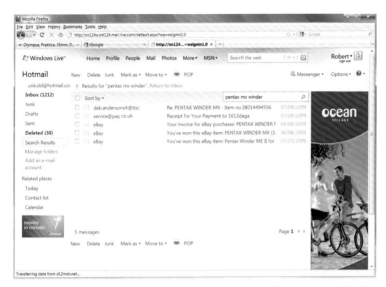

Fig.3.16 The Hotmail search system has also found the relevant Emails

with one checking through your Emails and the other providing a normal web search, so make sure that you use the right one. In the example of Figure 3.16 the Hotmail search facility has correctly located the Emails that contain the three specified search terms.

Customising

Modern web based Email systems provide the user with plenty of scope for customising the look of the program, and the way it functions. It is certainly well worthwhile exploring the options available from any part of the system that provides customisation facilities. There will often be separate facilities for controlling the appearance of the program, such as the screen colours, and the internal workings such as spam filtering and alerts. Figure 3.17 shows one of the customise pages for the Yahoo! Email system, and this is mainly concerned with the internal working of the program rather than its outward appearance.

If you are lucky there might be an option that permits the listing and reader panels to be split as left-hand and right-hand sections (Figure 3.18), rather than the default top and bottom arrangement. You will not

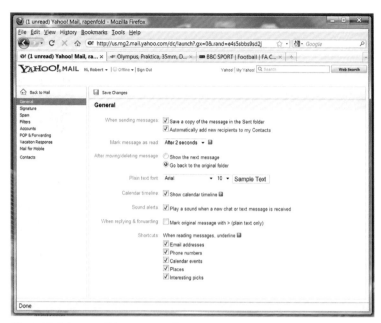

*Fig.3.17 It is possible to cusomise most web based Email systems.
          This is one of the settings pages for a Yahoo! Email account*

necessarily find that this makes the program easier to use, but this arrangement does seem to be more apposite for a small widescreen monitor. The "Classic" version of the program is still perhaps the most practical approach.

Modern web based Email programs are quite sophisticated, and there are more facilities available than can be covered here. There are usually facilities for importing contacts from other Email systems and programs for example. There is one big omission though. Although it used to be quite common for web based Email systems to have a facility for connecting to an Email program such as Outlook or Outlook Express, this no longer seems to be the case. It is sometimes possible by upgrading to an account where a subscription is paid, but it does not seem to be a feature of the free Email services. Most free web based Email systems are strictly web based, with no option to use a conventional Email program running on your PC.

Fig.3.18   There might be the option of splitting the main panel vertically instead of horizontally

Google Calendar

When in the Google Email system there is a link to the Google Calendar facility via a link near the top left-hand corner of the screen. Alternatively, it can be accessed by going to:

www.google.com/calendar

If not already signed in to the Google system, it will be necessary to sign in before proceeding further. Some information has to be provided on the first occasion that you use the Calendar software (Figure 3.19), and this is mainly required in order to ensure that the right time zone is used. Once into the Calendar program (Figure 3.20) it will default to displaying one week, with the cells for each day having one hour increments. However, the tabs also provide options for showing one day, a month, or four days. In Figure 3.21 the one month option has been selected, and this has one cell per day.

The Google Calendar program is not just for producing calendars, and it is really intended as a means of keeping track of your appointments, or "events" as they are called in Google terminology. There is more than one way of adding an event, but the most simple is to first double click

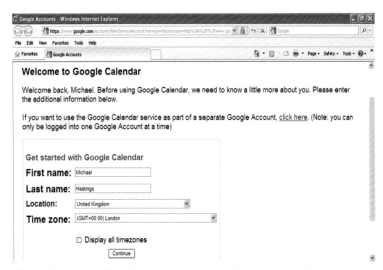

Fig.3.19   Some information has to be supplied prior to using the Google Calendar program for the first time

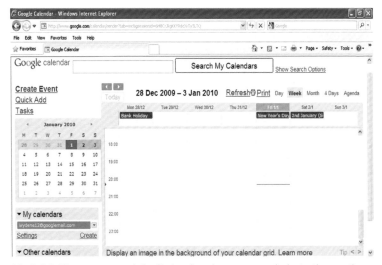

Fig.3.20   The program defaults to showing one week, but other options are available

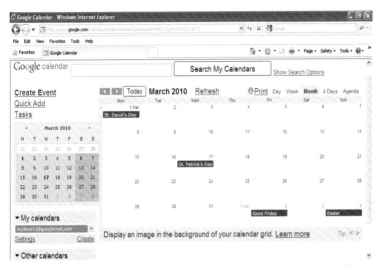

Fig.3.21 Here the tab for the one month dispay has been selected

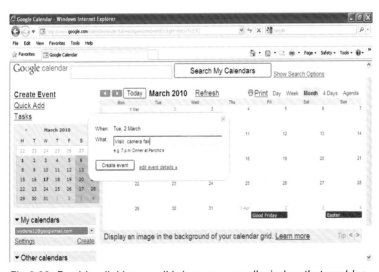

Fig.3.22 Double-clicking a cell brings up a small window that enables details of an event to be entered

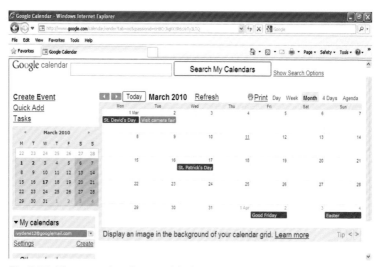

Fig.3.23 The event has been added successfully (it is the one coloured blue)

Fig.3.24 Activating the Create Event link brings up a form where details of the event can be entered

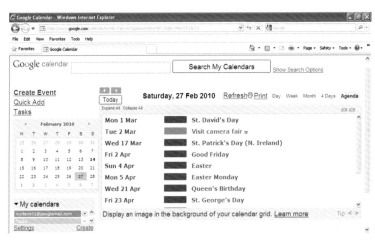

Fig.3.25 The Agenda tab produces a simple list of events

on the appropriate cell. This produces a pop-up window (Figure 3.22) where details of the event are added. In Figure 3.23 the new event has been added and is the one that is blue in colour. The red coloured events are the standard ones such as public holidays that have been added by the program. An alternative method is to activate the Create Event link near the top left-hand corner of the window, and then add the appropriate information to the form that appears (Figure 3.24).

The Agenda tab is very useful and it provides a simple list of events (Figure 3.25). It is worth investigating the Settings window (Figure 3.26), which is accessed via the link near the top right-hand corner of the normal window. This enables things such as the time and date format to be altered, the default view to be changed, and so on.

Microsoft Calendar

A similar facility is available from a Microsoft Email account such as one with Hotmail. Activating the Calendar link switches to this facility, and a small amount of information has to be entered when using the program for the first time (Figure 3.27). Tabs provide the option of viewing a day, a week, or one month, and the one month view is obtained by default. Double-clicking a cell brings up a small window where details of the event can be entered (Figure 3.28). In Figure 3.29 the new event has been added successfully, and it is the one in green. The blue events are

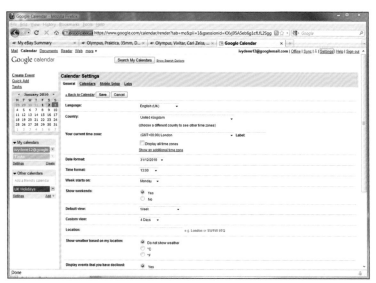

Fig.3.26   The Settings window enables things such as the time and
          date format to be changed

Fig.3.27   The Microsoft Calendar software also requires some
          information to be entered when it is used for the first time

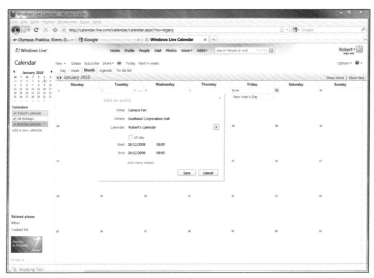

Fig.3.28 As before, double-clicking a cell brings up a small window so that details of the event can be entered

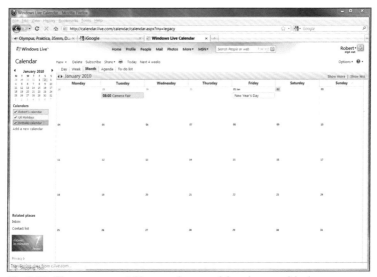

Fig.3.29 The new event (the one in green) has been added

Fig.3.30 An agenda is available via the appropriate tab

public holidays that are supplied by the program. The tabs provide an agenda (Figure 3.30), and there is also one for producing a "to do" list.

Spreadsheet

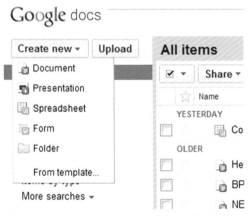

Fig.3.31 A Spreadsheet option is available in Google Docs

When in Google Docs there is a "Create new" menu near the top left-hand corner of the window, and the available options includes one for spreadsheets (Figure 3.31). Selecting this option brings up a conventional spreadsheet (Figure 3.32). This is actually quite a sophisticated piece of software, and a detailed description

Fig.3.32 The spreadsheet program is conventional in appearance

of it goes well beyond the scope of this book. If you need to use a spreadsheet program it is certainly worth trying this part of Google Docs.

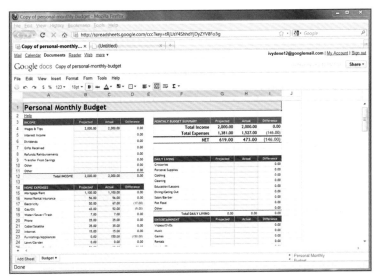

Fig.3.33 The spreadsheet program can be used with a template

Fig.3.34 Various types of chart are available

It can be used as a simple spreadsheet if that is all you need, but there are some advanced features as well. There are plenty of templates available for this software, and using something like "Google spreadsheet templates" in a search engine should provide numerous useful web pages. The spreadsheet of Figure 3.33 uses a monthly budgeting template. In many spreadsheet applications the ability to include charts without the need for a separate charting program is important. The current version of the Google spreadsheet program includes a very useful charting function (Figure 3.34).

Google Presentation

Another option under the "Create new" menu enables presentations to be produced. There is just one slide when the program is run, and as one would probably expect, this is a title page (Figure 3.35). Here a title and subtitle are added (Figure 3.36), but if preferred it is possible to delete this page and add a different type. Assuming you wish to use the default starting page, there is the usual range of editing tools, so the font, text size, text colour, etc., can be changed.

The next slide is added by either operating the "+" button near the top left-hand corner of the window, or by selecting "New slide" from the Slide

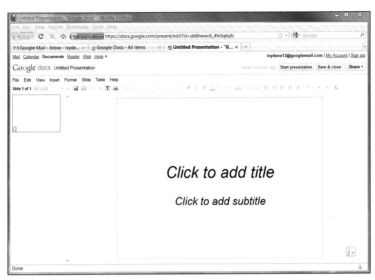

Fig.3.35 The presentation program starts with one page, which is a title page

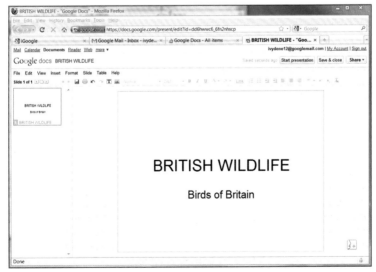

Fig.3.36 Here a suitable title and subtitle have been added

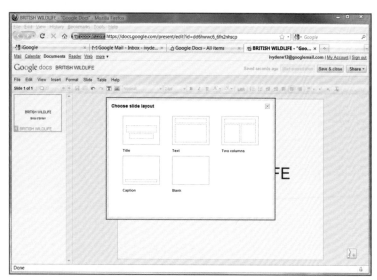

Fig.3.37 There is a choice of five layouts for slides

menu. You are then offered a choice of five different slide layouts (Figure 3.37). For this example I chose the Caption layout (Figure 3.38), and then added an image and a caption to the new slide (Figure 3.39). Images are added using the appropriate button in the toolbar, or by using the Insert menu. The latter also enables other objects such as text, videos, and tables to be added. The usual handles enable objects to be moved on the page and resized.

Bear in mind that when you use something like an image stored on your computer it is being uploaded to and stored on a Google server. Consequently, loading a high resolution image, or any other object that has a large file size, can be relatively slow. This is something that is to a large extent dependent on the upload speed of your Internet connection, but the upload rate is often very much less than the download speed.

Therefore, it is advisable to keep the file sizes of objects to the minimum that will do the job well. There is no point in uploading a ten megapixel image if it will only be used at one megapixel by a cloud application program. It is better to produce a smaller copy of about the right size and then upload that instead of the high resolution original. Always keep the higher resolution version of the image just in case you need a high quality version of it some time.

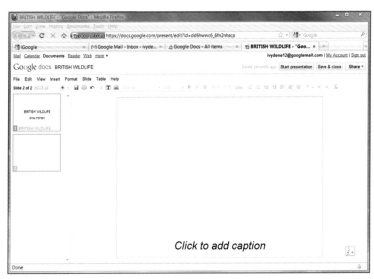

Fig.3.38 The new slide requires a caption and an image to be added

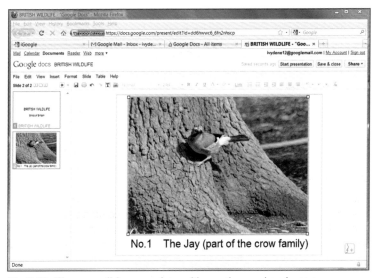

Fig.3.39 The new slide, complete with caption and an image

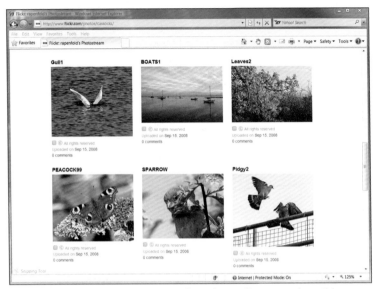

Fig.3.40 A netbook can handle online photo albums such as this example on Flickr.com

Another slide is then added, and the presentation is gradually built up. A thumbnail version of each slide appears in the left-hand column of the window, and the order of the slides can be changed by dragging their thumbnails to new positions. Right-clicking on one of the thumbnails brings up a menu that includes an option to delete it, move it up or down, or duplicate it. In general, adding content and editing it operates in standard Windows fashion, and it is quite easy to build up a presentation. The completed presentation can be downloaded in PDF, text, or PowerPoint format using the "Download as" option in the File menu.

The rest

It is not possible to cover the full range of cloud computing applications here, since the range is now so vast. Google Docs includes a facility for producing forms, there are sites that provide facilities for producing web sites or even complete web sites, and there are online photo album sites such Flickr.com (Figure 3.40), and so on. There is probably a cloud computing version of practically every popular type of application program.

Index